style on a budget

Emily Chalmers

with words by Ali Hanan

style on a budget

affordable ideas for a relaxed home

photography by Debi Treloar

RYLAND
PETERS
& SMALL

LONDON NEW YORK

First published in the USA in 2003
by Ryland Peters & Small, Inc.
519 Broadway
5th Floor
New York, NY 10012
www.rylandpeters.com

10 9 8 7 6 5 4 3 2 1

Library of Congress Cataloging-in-Publication Data

Chalmers, Emily.
  Style on a budget : affordable ideas for a relaxed
home / Emily Chalmers, with words by Ali Hanan ;
photography by Debi Treloar.
     p. cm.
  ISBN 1-84172-474-2
  1. Interior decoration. I. Hanan, Ali. II. Title.
  NK2115.C46 2003
  747--dc21
                                          2003009765

Printed and
bound in China.

Senior designer Catherine Griffin
Senior editor Henrietta Heald
Location research Claire Hector,
  Emily Chalmers
Production Patricia Harrington
Art director Gabriella Le Grazie
Publishing director Alison Starling
Stylist Emily Chalmers

contents

THIS PICTURE Color and pattern contrasts are used to add pizzazz to this dining room. With "rhapsody in blue" as the main theme, bright, bold patterns have been juxtaposed to give the room life and soul. Floor cushions do the same job as furniture—at half the price. In the background, a garland of floral lights introduces a festive touch.

LEFT AND BELOW LEFT Style on a budget involves thinking laterally about everyday objects. Here, handy handbags have become stylish storage for a little girl's bedroom, and a blue feather trim adds a touch of Africana to a simple lamp bought at a yard sale.

RIGHT Reclaim, recycle, reinvent. When hand-picking things for your home, don't ignore retired items, which in a new setting can become objects of desire. These simple French-style milk, coffee, and water pitchers are on the shelf and loving it.

introduction

Style on a Budget will help you create interior chic inexpensively. Packed with imaginative ideas, this book is a bible for the budget-conscious who also strive for style. Money, after all, can't buy good taste. Style is instinctive—and it can come at a snip as long as you have an eye for beauty as well as a bargain. As the interiors doyenne Andrée Putman once put it, "[To have] style is to see beauty in modest things."

To the owners of the homes illustrated in this book, vision is more important than cash. From a retro-style row house in London to a modern rustic home in Amsterdam, each interior has been selected for its savvy style. As you look at these pages, be inspired by the way the owners have ingeniously cherry-picked the things they live with to shape well-designed homes that don't need a designer label.

What makes cheap chic so desirable is how easy it is to achieve. From faking it to making it, there are countless ways to create a to-die-for interior at bargain prices. By scrimping in some areas, you can dine out in others. Spend your hard-earned cash on low-cost necessities and save for an investment buy—that single beautiful object or a floor that will last a lifetime.

LEFT **As it evolves over the years, a home becomes a living diary of the people who have dwelt in it and made their mark on the place. This engaging dog-on-wheels, for example—once a child's much-loved toy—is a witty memento.** RIGHT **In this wooden house-scape, natural highlights—a bowl of fruit and red roses in old liqueur bottles—give the room a visual kick.**

"Each one of these interiors has been so carefully considered," explains this book's stylist and researcher, Emily Chalmers. "To get luxury for less, you must be patient. Things don't turn up overnight. Be choosy and spend wisely." View objects laterally. Work magic. Innovate. Wave your style wand and turn a smooth door into a table-for-six. Who cares if it's not the real thing? Fake it. Veneer floors, for example, make fabulous forgeries.

What all the owners advise is to start with what you've got. Before renovating, begin the budget-friendly way by working with what you inherit. Peel back carpets, scuff off wallpapers, and hot-wash faded curtains. Reclaim vintage fabrics, original floorboards, and rustic-style brickwork. A fresh hand-sewn couch cover or a wash of bright new paint costs next to nothing, aside from a little time and effort.

That's what you need to get style on a shoestring. While chain stores have good-value pieces, the look is ubiquitous. Avoid the humdrum. Mix eras and styles by looking in less predictable places. For purse-friendly panache, follow your bargain-hunting instincts. Set your style sights on ethnic shops, secondhand stores, flea markets, yard sales, auctions, architectural salvage dealers, construction sites, even sidewalk throw-aways—the list is endless.

For style that's cheap, take inspiration from the interiors shown in this book. You will soon discover that you don't need to be wealthy to have a wealth of style.

THIS PICTURE **Tailor's models show off wooden plumber's beads, necklaces of dried chiles, and garish garlands of green crystal. They make a dramatic display in the hallway of this old house, where the floor has been brought back to life by a simple lick of paint.**
OPPOSITE, BELOW RIGHT **This simple table has both decorative and practical uses. It makes a pedestal for two large handsome vases and provides storage space beneath for a collection of trainers.**

the elements

color and pattern

Nothing changes a room as quickly as color. What's more, it is so easy to do. All it takes is a dash of blue or green, or a splash of pattern. You can transform a room in an evening with a coat of paint, or inject vibrancy with a striking pillow. And, even better, the materials you use won't make your wallet see red.

Color schemes not only influence mood, but you can use them—at low cost—to improve a room's whole shape and feel. Remember the decorator's rule of thumb: light colors expand a space, while dark colors reduce it. In a small room, use pale colors to make it appear larger, or create a den with dark colors. Another optical illusion is to make ceilings seem higher by painting the lower half of a room a darker color up to chest height and adding a lighter color up to the ceiling. Or, if you have an oddly shaped room, flatten it out visually with monochrome colors. By using color, you won't have to spend your cash on an architect—bargain!

To choose a scheme, think of things that you love. Are you inflamed by the deep aqua blues, razor-sharp whites, and fresh greens of Morocco? Or are you passionate about a particular era? Each decade has had its own color and pattern

OPPOSITE Sky-blue walls make a perfect background in this house of sunny contrasts. Every object displayed on the hutch, from the turquoise bowls to the raspberry-pink packaging, adds a shot of color.

THIS PAGE Geometric tiled floors, hot pink walls, and a blue rubber covering on the stairs create a mélange of color and pattern. The owner has made a feature of a coat rack, injecting dashes of aquamarine and orange into the entrance hall. To avoid visual overload, she has opted for a neutral white metal storage cabinet.

Give dull-looking objects a makeover
by adding a show-stopping cover. From
cushions to ironing boards, everyday
items simply need a new wrap.

palette. In the 1950s, pastels and florals reigned supreme; in the 1960s, brash colors – hot pinks, scarlet reds, and purples – and swirls dominated the mix; the 1970s loved geometrics and earthy colors; the 1980s splashed out on extravagant color schemes and gold-leaf fleur-de-lys; while the 1990s were all neutrals and textural patterns.

In the 21st century, you can choose any of these—and then add your own spin. Mix and match from different eras at low cost. Paint your walls in 1950s pastels—think baby pink, soft blue, or quiet green—and add contrasts with big square floor cushions or curtains sewn from vintage or reproduction retro fabrics to create pockets of pattern. Or buy geometric 1970s wallpaper in the colors of the decade—bright orange, earthy brown, and pea green—and contrast the pattern with a plain brown leather sofa.

OPPOSITE **While the overall scheme in this child's bedroom is restful, the circular candy-striped pillow on the bed and the shelf accessories introduce eye-catching contrasts.**

ABOVE LEFT **Injecting a little pattern pizzazz, these cheerful wall flowers become outstanding features of an otherwise utilitarian kitchen.**

ABOVE CENTER **Blue coat hangers have been teamed with a pink shirt against a door colored in soft lemon. The yellow provides the canvas, while the aqua blue and pink make the still-life painting on top of it.**

ABOVE **A rolltop bathtub looks drop-dead gorgeous in pastel pink against a white wall. Although paint is often used to spruce up walls, it can add swathes of color to a room and highlight pieces such as this tub.**

LEFT **One way to introduce bright hues without changing one iota of your interior is by taking advantage of nature's own color show: flowers. These pink roses displayed in delicate Moroccan tea glasses represent a simple, stunning example of flower power.**

BELOW LEFT **Era-ureka! Pillow fabrics in chinoiserie style meet swinging 1970s wallpaper. A combination of eras and styles in this Dutch house creates an eye-stopping interior. To find similar wallpapers, look for vintage prints in the bins of secondhand stores or new wallpaper swatchbooks. With the recent wallpaper revival, many companies are doing fabulous reprints of hip hits.**

THIS PICTURE **Out-of-sight becomes sight friendly. Chests, closets and drawers in funky colors can be used to hide all sorts of clutter and eyesores. By lowering the ceiling, these London homeowners have created ample storage space behind sliding cherry-red doors.**

RIGHT **One wide taupe horizontal stripe brings a brushstroke of modernity to this neutral dining room.**

Whereas the 1990s was a whitewash of neutral colors and white, white paint, one of the trends to emerge in the first decade of the new century is the revival of wallpaper—and, with it, pattern. Trawl secondhand stores that hoard rolls of vintage papers, or hunt through the latest catalogs for the nouveau ethnic designs—chinoiserie styles, African designs, modern florals—that are rolling off the presses and onto walls.

For a quick, low-cost update, give your walls a fresh coat of white paint—two coats of brilliant white will do—for that minimalist feel, and then paper just a single wall.

ABOVE **Color and texture work like yin and yang. In this kitchen, ruddy tiles make a crossword-style backdrop for somber Provençal-style cooking pots.**
ABOVE RIGHT **Far from a featureless passageway, this would-be wallflower of a stairwell is the belle of the house with its sunny-yellow 1970s wallpaper.**
OPPOSITE, LEFT **Instead of organizing your books alphabetically by author in the style of a library, order them according to height and color and turn them into eye-catching features.**
OPPOSITE, RIGHT **A ruby-red bead curtain delineates space and brings in a splash of warmth. In front of it, an oriental floral paper lightshade, bought for a song, brings in a sky-blue contrast.**

If you discover a busy pattern or want to paint a stencil, don't overdo it. The trick is to think about highlights and contrasts. Combine patterns and plains to get the right balance. Add different tones for interest and bring them to life with contrasts. For example, blue blends well with green, but is given a visual kick with a touch of orange; brown and taupe make harmonious partners, but the partnership can be spiced up with turquoise and mustard yellows.

The key to getting the overall scheme right is good planning. To make the process easier, use a stylist's trick and create a swatch book. Cut samples or take Polaroids of the fabric, carpets, or curtains you are intending to buy, then visit a hardware store to

Combine subtly different shades of color for interest, and bring these to life with contrasts.

find the paint to match. If you are using paint, you can save yourself time and money by purchasing testers. Paint a square yard of wall space in your chosen test shade and observe how the color looks at different times of the day as the light in the room changes.

While color and pattern live on in paint and fabrics, don't forget about accessories. One particularly eye-catching trick (look at *Elle Decoration* magazine) is to display accessories by hanging them. For a shot of pattern, pick your favorite dress, shirt, or skirt and suspend it from a colorful coathanger over a wall or door. This would work equally well with the rest of your wardrobe. Hang out your handbags or string your necklaces from nails or hooks.

OPPOSITE ABOVE, LEFT AND RIGHT **All good canvases are neutral. In a room with soft blue walls, the eye is automatically drawn towards the sculptural fireplace and the curvaceous silhouettes of painted wooden chairs; the shelves are a stage for the sculptural forms of teapots, cups, saucers, and mugs.**
OPPOSITE BELOW, LEFT **An ingenious way to bring in color is to display your glorious garments. Hang them for highlights and for ideas. For example, the jumpsuit inspired the stunning color combination shown in the picture on this page.**
OPPOSITE BELOW, RIGHT **Floors, doors, walls and furniture—indeed, virtually any hard surfaces—are suitable for painting.**
RIGHT **Horizontal slats of color revive the otherwise plain walls in this child's bedroom.**

Remember nature, which has some of the best color and textures available. Buy big, colorful, long-stemmed flowers and put them center-stage in any room for a huge shot of color. Instead of traditional vases, improvise with cheap containers such as plastic buckets, wine coolers, and bottles. For long-lasting looks, plant bulbs in teacups or cereal bowls on a sunny window ledge or buy flowering potted plants. Make your own fresh floral garlands—simply buy carnations or other flower heads, thread them onto a long, colorful string, and dangle them from the ceiling.

Don't be reluctant to experiment. And, if you get bored with a particular color or the look you want doesn't seem to be working in the way you intended, color is easy to change with a flick of a paintbrush. Pattern works in a similar way. For a new feel, simply introduce different pillow covers, bedspreads, throws, or rugs. A plain backdrop allows you to be fickle. Change from geometric to paisley, or from paisley to floral. Create.

top tips for color and pattern

MAKE THE MOST OF WHAT'S THERE For earthy tones, strip back surfaces. Underneath you may find original brickwork, floorboards, or old flagstones, which cost nothing to you but look priceless.

GO NEUTRAL AND NATURAL The cheapest schemes often use the colors of raw materials—such as wooden floors and whitewashed walls—as a canvas; with a neutral backdrop, patterns and colors can come and go as you please.

TREAT YOUR INTERIOR LIKE YOUR WARDROBE Spend on accessorizing colors and patterns as you would on your own clothes; a new cushion or a swathe of vintage cloth often costs half the price of pair of shoes.

USE COLOR TO ENHANCE ARCHITECTURE Rather than spending thousands removing walls, renovating windows, and lowering ceilings, use color to create visual effects and maximize the potential of a room.

BE INSPIRED As interior doyenne Andrée Putman says, "I have no recipe for how to combine things. But you must be sincere. And if you are, strangely, it will succeed." The rule is to avoid convention. Mix patterns and colors that work for you.

fabrics

Soften a hard edge. Provide texture and color, warmth and comfort. Partition a room. Gently filter light. Is there anything fabrics can't do? Even better, there are many fabrics that can be picked up for a song.

As with most other things in the home, when it comes to fabrics it pays to invest in quality. Usually, this means natural fibers. For example, it is a false economy to buy cheap dishtowels made of a polyester and cotton mix, which inevitably shrink. Instead, save your cash for second-hand linen dishtowels. Why? Linen is an incredible fiber. Moisture-resistant, soft, and strong—three times as strong when wet—it is the perfect material for dishtowels, napkins, tablecloths, and sheets.

Wool, too, outstrips its synthetic imitators. It can be bent up to 30,000 times without being damaged—making it ideal for floor rugs and couch throws. Acting as a natural insulator, wool also preserves heat and soaks up noise. For inexpensive rugs, exercise your bartering skills at Persian shops or markets, or buy sheepskins and blankets from chain stores.

One important feature of natural fibers is that they "breathe"—which, when it comes to bed linen, helps the body regulate its temperature. If you can't find secondhand linen sheets, try new

OPPOSITE, ABOVE AND BELOW LEFT **Fabrics that cost next to nothing can look a million dollars. For example, a piece of fur casually tossed over an old Turkish cushion makes a glamorous feature, and a ruddy felt basket provides smart storage for scarves.**

OPPOSITE, ABOVE RIGHT **A thick curtain, linen on one side and felt on the other, is suspended by a sturdy rod running through eyelets.**

OPPOSITE, BELOW RIGHT **Liven up an old dishtowel or rejuvenate a blanket with a trim. The great thing about fabrics is that they allow you to ad lib. Sew on buttons, sequins, ribbons, beads, or shells to make a Cinderella pillow the belle of the hall.**

THIS PAGE **Disguise an old sofa in style. Here, the sofa has been dressed up, softened with an old sheet, and highlighted with mix-'n'-match striped pillows.**

THIS PAGE **From the little notebooks propped up on a windowsill, all wearing flower-print dust jackets, to the soft cotton bag hanging from a doorknob, florals give these interiors a fresh, pretty look. Piles of fabrics, like piles of books, make a fabulous feature. It pays to choose natural fabrics because they endure more wear and tear than synthetic fabrics, as any antique linen towel attests.**

THIS PAGE **Combined and contrasted with contemporary pieces, the floral pillows and vinyl-coated tablecloth give these interiors a modern country feel. Rather than being fusty, florals, when set against clean white backgrounds, look fresh and soft. The fabulous thing about fabrics is you can change them with the seasons, as long as the canvas remains neutral, as here. This flowery look is an ideal style for spring.**

Egyptian cotton sheets, considered to be the best quality (at the best price). Rough-weave fabrics such as earthy burlap, horsehair, and hemp not only breathe, but also let the light through. For chic room dividers or window covers, buy these pieces as strips or panels from fabric or craft stores.

Natural fabrics, unless dyed, have a limited color range: stone, cream, chocolate brown, taupe, which is fine for a mother-earth palette. For a little rock 'n' roll, scour secondhand stores for off-beat fabrics—vintage bedspreads, dresses, jeans, and coats—at rock-bottom prices. All you need is a bit of imagination and a sewing machine. With scissors and thread, you can transform these pieces into floor cushions, sofa covers, curtains, or patchwork blankets.

Keep your eyes peeled for classics such as faded florals, tweeds, cool corduroys, and stone-washed denims. You are bound to find fabric friends to match your style. Retro lovers will search out vintage fabrics from the 1950s, 1960s, and 1970s; soft modernists will favor faded florals and denims; traditionalists will covet tweeds; and those who love exoticana must seek anything from Indonesian batiks to Chinese silks and West African prints.

Ethnic shops are ideal hunting grounds for funky fabrics such as hot-pink, gold-rimmed Indian saris and Samoan tapa cloth that do so much to spice up an interior. A sari, for example, could become a vibrant table runner or a beautiful wall hanging; to transform a sari into a gauzy curtain, simply sew a casing and thread it on a rod—when the breeze catches it, the fabric will billow and sigh.

Otherwise, recycle what you've got. A cheap way to make soft-to-cuddle cushions is to hot-wash your old wool knits to make felt, and sew them into

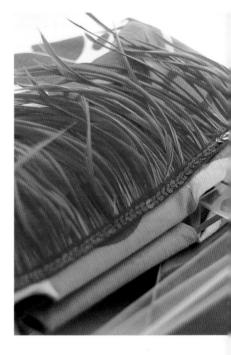

ABOVE **An exotic pattern meets subtle stripes in this arresting display of pillows. As such a bold combination illustrates, fabrics don't necessarily have to match to work together. The rule of thumb in fashion is to put everything into the melting pot of your own taste—and have the courage of your convictions.**
ABOVE RIGHT **Fabrics also make instant accessories, as shown by these cotton cloths draped casually over knobs on a kitchen cabinet door.**
RIGHT **The key to achieving true style on a budget is to keep your eyes open for materials in their natural habitats—think of your grandmother's collection of curtains, shawls, and bedspreads—then recycle and adapt them with trimmings such as sequins and feathers, which can be used to add texture and color.**

THIS PICTURE **Ethnic fabrics such as this beautiful bright sari and the chinoiserie-style cushion covers recall lavish cultures and exotic lands. Search out examples of global style in flea markets and ethnic stores, or collect swathes of textiles during your overseas travels. Think laterally about their uses: a sari could make an exotic, ethereal window cover as well as a cheap-'n'-chic child's bedcover.**

top tips for fabrics

LET NATURAL FIBERS RULE Synthetics often lack the resilience of natural fibers. Favor wool, linen, cotton, silks, and other long-lasting fibers, which are breathable, durable, and sensuous.

BE INNOVATIVE Don't confine fabrics to bedrooms. Use swathes of heavy rough-weave fabrics as room dividers; hang long dyed-muslin panels over windows instead of curtains; stretch striped canvas around an old lampshade frame.

LOOK IN ODD PLACES Fabulous fabrics may have unlikely origins—your grandmother's shawls or your latest cast-offs, for example. Trawl secondhand stores for old curtains, dresses, tweed jackets, and sew them into—well, anything!

CHANGE WITH THE SEASONS Dress your home with different textures and fabrics to reflect the time of year: fake fur and wool for winter; voile and cotton for summer.

MATCH THE DURABLE AND THE DECORATIVE Making floor cushions? Use a sturdy fabric such as denim or suede for a backing and a cotton floral pattern for the front.

covers. You can change an old sheet into a stylish tablecloth by the simple application of a colorful dye. Or try the reverse: turn a lace tablecloth into a bedcover or use as a window covering to diffuse sunrays into cobweblike patterns. Don't forget that fabrics can also revitalize lackluster bathrooms. Instead of buying dull white bath towels from chain stores, use colorful beach towels to inject a little dash into your bathroom.

Fabrics are your home's clothes, and, like your own wardrobe, they can change with the seasons. Pillow covers, throws, sheets, and blankets can come and go with the weather. Create a warm, curl-up atmosphere in your living room each winter with fake fur throws, burlap shades and second-hand checked wool blankets. As spring comes, pack them away—it's time for floral patchwork cushions, light muslin curtains, and denim throws. Fabric is fantastically flexible. No other material used in the home does so much for so little.

window treatments

Treat yourself to a window treatment —and make it beautiful. Windows are a room's best asset. Harness the power of light with economical curtains, shades, shutters, and screens. Depending on the season and your need for privacy, there are plenty of shoestring solutions to covering windows with style.

If you need privacy without loss of light, choose light-diffusing window covers. Homemade covers are kind to wallets. For example, take an old rollup shade and puncture it with rows of holes to let the rays dapple through. Or create a play of diffused light and color with dyed voile strips. First, buy three lengths of voile (or similar fabric) to match the height of your window and finish the seams. Dye two of the strips rust red and one burnt orange. Using contrasting ribbon, tie them to screw-in hooks and hang them with the orange strip in the middle.

Fabrics such as voile, organdy, or old lace, or Japanese blinds, are gentle on the purse. If you want a private space only at certain times of day, try using old-fashioned screens, which double as room dividers. Another solution, which combines diffusion with total blackout, are blinds and shutters, now available at reasonable prices

THIS PAGE AND RIGHT Opaque coverings such as voiles, silks, and lace diffuse the light while shielding interiors from intrusive gazes. It is easy to find cheap lengths of these fabrics in fabric stores, but don't forget that you can reclaim and reuse old sheets, lace shawls, and former tablecloths. A bobble trim adds an edge. RIGHT, INSETS It's curtains for expensive curtains. For a neat finish, simply use yacht hooks bought from a chandler and string up army tent fabric on a metal wire (left); or use traditional curtain eyes and sling them along a painted broomstick, wire, or mop handle (right). The curtain in the right inset is a mixture of linen for looks and wool for warmth.

Nothing beats a
natural wash of bright
sunlight on bare walls,
fading from a sharp
white to rose pink as
twilight comes.

THIS PICTURE A length of sari fabric with a rhythmic pattern diffuses a beautiful dappled light. Former bedspreads, wall hangings, scarves, vintage quilts, and sequined saris make equally luxurious light filters.

OPPOSITE, LEFT Instead of shopping at traditional places for blinds, explore alternative sources such as ethnic stores. From Japanese rice-paper blinds to this Middle Eastern slatted-cane rollup shade, you could find cheap covers at prices to light up your life.

OPPOSITE, BELOW RIGHT Horizontal slats of lights diffused through a white aluminum blind make a room seem wider, while vertical slats would make a ceiling appear higher. Venetian blinds allow illumination varying from total blackout to diffused light.

OPPOSITE, SMALL PICTURE, LEFT An old blanket hangs at the window in this stairwell.

OPPOSITE, SMALL PICTURE, RIGHT This window cover is elegantly strung out along an old piece of pipe (a length of scaffold pipe would also do) by means of fabric loops. Such loops are easy to sew, but curtains like this can be found for a song in chain stores.

LEFT A pleated cotton shade allows light a look in but disappoints prying eyes. Plants in an outside windowbox also provide a discreet screen.
BELOW LEFT Who needs blinds when you could replace them with strings of beads, artificial flower heads, or mother-of-pearl circles like these?
THIS PICTURE Among the stylish alternatives to traditional blinds are low-cost pleated papers.

RIGHT **One straightforward way to create a window screen is to use nature's own sun-swallowing blinds: long-stemmed flowers, tall houseplants, or climbers. Arrange vases of flowers such as tiger lilies, tall roses, and geraniums on a windowsill or create a swirly verdant cover with thick ivy or fragrant jasmine. A windowsill is the perfect site for plants that love sun, including herbs such as bushy basil and willowy mint.**

from chain stores. At night they give total blackout, but by day they can create architectural illusions: blinds allow horizontal slashes of light to enter a room, making it expand, while shutters let in vertical strips, making the ceiling appear higher.

For draft-free winter coziness or for rooms penetrated by the glare of streetlights, total exclusion of light is desirable. You don't need budget-busting velvet curtains to achieve this. Instead, use thick, chunky alternatives such as old bedspreads, blankets, strips of denim, squares of felt, suede, an old rug attached to a wire with strong clips, or vintage quilts strung up with ribbon. If you want absolute darkness, sew blackout fabric, available from most fabric stores, to the window side.

There is one final option, which costs nothing: use no covering at all. Go for the "Emperor's New Clothes" and leave windows as the architectural kings that they are. Nothing beats a natural wash of bright sunlight, fading from a sharp white to a rose-colored light on bare walls as twilight comes. Stained-glass windows are often better left uncovered, too, since they create their own equally dramatic play of light while providing privacy. After all, windows are often the most striking feature in a room, so why hide them?

top tips for window treatments

RECYCLE Reuse or buy old shawls, bedspreads, rugs, and blankets. Tie them onto screw-in hooks or sew the top section over an old broomstick or curtain pole, and tie back with ribbon or rope.

MAKE YOUR OWN Fabrics that don't fray take away the need for a sewing machine. Alternatively, show off your loose ends by gently fraying away an inch or two. Use lengths of sari to fit long windows; buy suede skins, cut into squares, and tack them together; or string up antique lace tablecloths.

THINK SECONDHAND Curtains often turn up at yard sales and in secondhand stores. You may spot a pair that simply need dry cleaning.

HAVE A FLUTTER ON A SHUTTER Architectural salvage yards are a good source of wooden shutters, shades, and blinds. Sand and repaint them before installing.

SHOP AT ETHNIC STORES Eastern cultures have their own ways of treating light: Japanese rice-paper blinds blend in with minimalist interiors; Chinese folding screens, either painted or made from silk fabric, make a beautiful addition to any interior.

furniture

Stylish, functional, affordable: pieces of furniture can be all these and more. From inflatable plastic sofas to customized flat-pack stools, you need to sharpen your instincts for a bargain. Items can be freestanding (ideal for urban nomads) or tailor-made and built-in (perfect for people who are firmly settled), but neither need cost you dear.

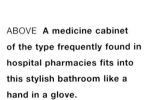

When it comes to furniture, it pays to acquire a few key items that have been chosen for their quality, particularly a proper bed—after all, we spend a third of our lives asleep. If you buy a good bed now, you won't have to change it for at least ten years.

Investment buys should always be freestanding. Once you have put your money where your comfort is and bought, for example, an ultra-soft armchair, the piece can become your living companion, moving with you from place to place.

Another asset is a decent leather sofa, which, if it is a classic, will actually increase in value over the years and end up outliving you. Vintage leather sofas and chairs such as 1930s club armchairs perfectly illustrate the value of quality. As long as they are classic pieces and manufactured from good, strong—usually natural—materials, they will last and last. Strong, wipeable, polish-it-up leather (even white leather) is also one of the few couch coverings that ages with grace.

ABOVE A medicine cabinet of the type frequently found in hospital pharmacies fits into this stylish bathroom like a hand in a glove.

ABOVE LEFT This curvaceous, low-slung couch provides a neutral background for covers, cushions, and throws. These accessories can come and go to satisfy the owner's mood or the changing seasons. A piece like this is an investment.

LEFT If you are not fortunate enough to inherit beautiful objects like those that make up this "still-life in furniture," track down your own in secondhand stores, junk yards, and architectural salvage stores.

THIS PAGE **In this peaceful bedroom, white walls, ceiling, and floor make a blank canvas for the bed-as-sculpture. A floral patchwork quilt softens the industrial-style frame, while two matching lamps flank the bed in stark contrast to the reclaimed side cabinets.**

Architectural salvage
yards and thrift stores
often have old pieces
that need no more than
love, attention, and
a coat of paint.

OPPOSITE PAGE **Items from different eras have been combined to add interest to this contemporary London house; here a 1970s brown-glass ashtray sits beside a 1950s Draylon lounge suite. Stylish retro armchairs and low coffee tables in good condition like these can often be found in secondhand furniture stores.**
THIS PICTURE **An old pair of curvy secondhand chairs has been recovered for a modern dining room. Re-upholstering or sewing new covers—think canvas, terrycloth, or burlap for a hard-wearing material—is a low-cost way to give furniture a new lease on life.**

THIS PICTURE **Against a contemporary white canvas, old pieces such as a large refectory table have been resurrected. A former church pew provides seating, while in the background weather-beaten wooden boards make rustic-style shelving.**

OPPOSITE, ABOVE RIGHT **This chair is as famous as it is ubiquitous. An early example of bent plywood, it was designed at the start of the 20th century by Michael Thonet. By 1930, 50 million chairs had been produced —and the chair is still being manufactured today.**

OPPOSITE, BELOW, LEFT TO RIGHT **Cheap chic places to perch include a plastic child's chair with an African-inspired design, an old straw-seated stool revived by a lick of white paint, and a metal workstool softened by a striped cushion.**

If you don't have much spare cash, give serious thought to secondhand furniture, which usually scrubs up well. For example, it is easy (and relatively cheap) to give secondhand fabric-covered couches a new lease on life by having them reupholstered. Choose a hard-wearing fabric such as striped canvas. Or, if the couch is in good shape, simply sew a couple of colored slipcovers to fit, changing them when the mood takes you—or as small sticky hands or food and drink spillages add their own overtones to the orchestra of cover colors.

Unless you own your own home, avoid built-in furniture, which you won't be able to take with you when you move. If you do have a home of your own, the good news is that shelves, armoires, and cabinets can be built without wallet-shattering consequences. Built-in storage is often the only way to finish the jigsaw of an oddly shaped room. Get a carpenter to install cut-to-fit shelves or built-in seating with low-cost medium-density fiberboard or rustic recycled wood. What makes a piece of furniture stylish is often in the eye of the beholder—or what it's teamed with. If your built-in cabinet lacks chic, jazz it up with sleek streamlined aluminum handles or pretty teardrop plastic knobs.

When shopping for furniture, look anywhere and everywhere. A good place to start is the mall. For a Pop feel, go for fun items such as the mod-looking inflatable pieces found in all sorts

top tips for furniture

THINK INVESTMENT BUYS For your own comfort and sanity, invest in a few key portable pieces such as a decent, decadent bed and a sink-into sofa. When you move on, these pieces can go with you.

SHOP IN THE CHAIN Interior stores stock a range of styles that are already chic, such as retro reproduction pieces, or adaptable (don't judge a couch by its cover—as long as it's a good solid style, you can disguise it with a new cover or throw).

LOOK OUT FOR THE UNEXPECTED Next time you are in your nearest Chinatown or Arabic enclave, look out for ethnic pieces. An oriental paper lampshade or an Arabic coffee table adds an exotic dash.

DON'T DISMISS TAILOR-MADE Built-in furniture does not have to be expensive as long as it is made from economical materials such as composite board. Add a thick coat of paint and accessorize.

BE RESOURCEFUL Trawl secondhand stores and yard sales, keeping your eyes open for general pieces that you can adopt and adapt.

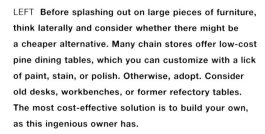

LEFT Before splashing out on large pieces of furniture, think laterally and consider whether there might be a cheaper alternative. Many chain stores offer low-cost pine dining tables, which you can customize with a lick of paint, stain, or polish. Otherwise, adopt. Consider old desks, workbenches, or former refectory tables. The most cost-effective solution is to build your own, as this ingenious owner has.

of style stores. Mainstream interior stores often have great retro designs at purse-friendly prices. Look out for Robin Day plastic bucket seats and Verner Panton rugs, for example.

Then there is style beyond the mall. Ethnic furniture stores are full of treasures awaiting discovery, including Moroccan leather poofes, woven African footstools, and in-laid mother-of-pearl Chinese side tables.

Architectural salvage yards and secondhand stores often have old pieces that just need a little love and attention and a coat of paint. The adage "one person's trash is another person's treasure" also holds true—have a look in dumpsters and examine sidewalk cast-offs.

Otherwise, be inventive and construct your own furniture. For example, rustic stools can be made from old tree trunks picked up in a salvage yard. Strip off the bark, sand the wood, stain, varnish and—*voila!* Or make a dining table by perching an old door on two trestles and covering it with a white linen tablecloth. Nail old railroad ties together to make a rustic coffee table; use former wine boxes as shelves; put velvet cushions on wooden crates to make living-room stools. The key to embellishing your home with stylish budget furniture is lateral thinking.

THIS PICTURE Antique pieces such as this leather-clad club chair from the 1930s are an investment. Leather ages with grace, keeping its looks from decade to decade. If you find an old piece that you love, hold on to it because it may appreciate with time. ABOVE RIGHT AND BELOW RIGHT Try the mall for contemporary stylish items on the cheap, such as this glass table top and the space-saving nest of tables.

storage and display

Space is one of your home's most prized possessions. When you free it up, you realize how much room you really have. Whatever your budget, the secret to good storage is to create a place for everything and put everything back where it belongs. It takes no more than a little ingenuity for all your belongings to find a home—and with style.

Good storage comes in many shapes and sizes, and calls for many degrees of access. It's up to you to judge what to display. Bury old school books deep in an attic or under a stairwell, but keep aesthetically pleasing objects out in the open.

One of the cheapest—and easiest—ways to create storage space is to go Zen, throwing away all the junk in your possession and keeping only beautiful or useful things. Be ruthless: if you haven't worn an item for the past year, donate it to someone who will wear it. Swap books for cash or exchange old CDs. This process should make your storage problem seem much less of a mountain. As you finish filing your possessions, keep out the pieces that mean most to you. The rest can remain discreetly tucked away in cabinets and on shelves. With your possessions pared back to a minimum, you know that what you still own is what you really love.

ABOVE **In a former life, these practical trolleys, now piled high with soft fresh towels and bedding, were used for transporting items around a factory.**
ABOVE LEFT **This galvanized-steel storage system is equally at home outdoors and in.**
LEFT **Old wooden filing drawers have been given a new lease on life as storage for odds and ends.**
OPPOSITE **A bank of cabinets makes the most of limited storage space in this small London apartment, enabling the owners to stash most of their possessions, including the television, neatly out of sight. Painted in a variety of neutral tones, the cabinet doors blend harmoniously with one another.**

There are two main types of storage: built-in and movable. If you are an urban nomad, make movable storage one of your investment buys—think antique suitcases and vintage wooden tea chests. Such pieces often last for years, transporting precious belongings from home to home, and perhaps doubling as furniture when you settle. It's an old tradition: from the 17th century in Europe, when families immigrated to a new world, all-purpose chests would be used to contain their entire belongings—and after the destination had been reached, would double as beds or dining tables.

Movable storage means flexible storage, and it can also mean stylish storage. For example, a stack of old briefcases in cracked leather, a knot of red-lacquer Chinese jewelry boxes and a painted bookshelf turned into a home-office photo gallery can become show-stopping features in their own right. Build your own for next to

ABOVE **A capacious old medicine cabinet blends in with the clean feel of this contemporary bathroom. Storage pieces intended for public places such as restaurants, retail outlets, hospitals, and libraries can often work equally well in home spaces.**

TOP **Mobile shelves fastened to a metal frame make flexible storage for spices and other ingredients. This kind of shelving—which allows everything to be kept in clear view—is ideal in a kitchen, where tasks often need to be carried out at speed.**

ABOVE LEFT **Sculptural stainless-steel pots, pans, and kitchen utensils line up elegantly, swinging from butchers' hooks.**

OPPOSITE **A factory trolley makes a handy home for pairs of shoes. With this kind of storage, you can easily see what you've got and where it is at a glance—which makes it much simpler to be well organized.**

THIS PICTURE **This enormous storage cabinet doesn't quite reach the ceiling. A cabinet designed this way deceives the eye into perceiving the room as more spacious than it is.**

LEFT **A rack of beautiful trays and dishes adds color, texture, and form to a kitchen. Blending practicality and aesthetics, this storage solution shows off objects that should not hide behind closed doors.**

RIGHT **If you have matching sets of plates, and cups and saucers, display them on open shelves.**

BELOW RIGHT **To exploit every inch of kitchen space, delicate teacups have been hung out of harm's way on wall hooks, adding a sculptural element to the room.**

nothing. For rough-edged industrial chic, mount a wooden plank on stacks of bricks. All these solutions look good and house your precious booty, but can move on when you do.

Built-in storage—invented in the early 19th century—may not be transportable, but it can be made to look superbly stylish at little expense. Use your handy skills to construct cabinets and shelves, or employ a carpenter to make these pieces out of low-cost materials such as medium-density fiberboard and recycled woods. Many chain stores have flat-pack off-the-shelf units—shelves, drawers, cabinets—at affordable prices.

The great thing about built-in storage is that you can blend it seamlessly with your interior. For example, a floor-to-ceiling cabinet occupying an entire wall is a great way to create a huge storage space. Either make a feature of it, as shown on page 45, or paint it in a color to match the rest of your room and use sturdy push-click cabinet hardware so the cabinet looks just like part of the room (see page 49).

Built-in storage can make the most of the "dead" spaces found in oddly shaped rooms—if you have a triangular alcove, you could square it off by putting in a corner cabinet or make a feature of it with shelves. Such storage can also be multipurpose. In your living room, for example, you could install built-in seating along one wall and put a hinged cover on the top to create storage underneath for videos, CDs, and books.

When you sift through your possessions there will always be a special knot of items that cry out

Fototoestel

Landkaarten

Post Wim

Ansichtkaarten

Fietsspullen Wim

Wim Allerle

Agenda's Joos

Wim Allerlei

oiletspullen Joos

Schoenpoets

etspullen Allerlei

Toiletspullen Joos

Medicijnen

tyling Lapjes

Kantoorspullen

Styling Allerl

LEFT AND INSET **Neatly labeled plastic storage boxes, stacked from floor to ceiling, are the key to order in this efficient-looking home office.** OPPOSITE, RIGHT, ABOVE AND BELOW **Former wine boxes come to the storage party. A wallet-friendly way to combine storage and display, this idea needed only a little investment of time and a lot of wine drinking. The boxes have been transformed into showcases for colorful kitchen herbs and fabulous flowers.** OPPOSITE, LEFT, ABOVE AND BELOW **Storage is either stationary or movable. This vegetable rack is mounted on castors, making it easy to maneuver around the kitchen to the spot where it is needed. Another advantage of storage of this kind is that it can move with you. The metal slats also allow stocktaking to be done at a glance.**

The secret of good storage is to create a place for everything and put everything in its place.

to be displayed. Whether they are personal mementoes, such as photographs of loved ones, or collections of favorite objects, these are your own treasures and should be paraded with panache. To make them showstoppers, avoid convention and predictability. Rather than arranging your photo frames on a mantelpiece in time-honored fashion, clip them to a string and hang it along a wall—or transform a stairwell or a toilet wall into a "hall of fame" and put up large black-and-white portraits of your nearest and dearest.

Display your gorgeous things in disused or alternative spaces: stack books and magazines along a hallway instead of in fusty bookcases; dot flowers in Moroccan glass tea cups up the stairs; hang your Noel Coward-style dressing gown in the living room.

Instead of simply perching pieces on ledges, be original about how you present them. One way to economize on space and flaunt

THIS PICTURE **Arranged along this industrial-style record storage unit is a mixture of shapes, colors, and objects. Here, simple display has become a gallery of beautiful things, each one basking in its own glory.**
OPPOSITE, LEFT **If you own beautiful clothes, don't hide them. Make a feature of your robes, as this owner has. And, of course, if you hang your glad rags on a pole, you won't need to pay for a closet to put them in, leaving more to spend on the clothes themselves.**
OPPOSITE, CENTER **Far from their natural home on the floor, these wooden shoe-shapers make elegant hooks for bags in another storage-and-display double act.**
OPPOSITE, RIGHT **A magazine rack goes to the wall. This café-style newspaper and magazine holder saves precious floor space.**

your beautiful things is to hang them. All sorts of functional—and aesthetic—pieces look stunning when strung from racks, hooks, or rods. Collections of copper pots and pans hung from butchers' hooks in a kitchen bring together practicality and artistry. Other ways to create eye-catching features include suspending utensils from rods and dangling tea cups from wall hooks.

In a bedroom, clothes don't always have to be locked away behind closed doors. A clothes rod, for example, is a quietly simple way to make a feature of your clothes collection. Handbags, scarves, belts, and evening bags draped from hooks nailed to walls not only make a stunning display but are also very easy to access.

Display the things you love, but give them room to breathe. Remember, a clutch of exquisite small stones collected from the seashore looks more arresting on an otherwise bare shelf than lost amid a crowd of other bits 'n' bobs. A small cluster is more effective than a load of clutter.

top tips for storage and display

REINVENT, RECYCLE, AND REUSE Some ordinary household items offer great storage solutions. Jelly jars and plastic ice-cream boxes, for example, make good airtight food containers, while old doctors' bags and toolboxes make alternative containers for toiletries, sewing kits, scarves, gloves, and hats.

"CREATE" SPACE Instead of a wall, install a floor-to-ceiling storage system, accessible from both sides, built from composite board. Or square off a corner with a triangular cabinet or shelf rack and "create" space.

MAKE A FEATURE OF STORAGE Get hold of simple cardboard boxes or former fruit crates or shoe-boxes, and customize them with paint or stylish wrapping paper, or cover with vintage wallpaper.

OPT FOR ALTERNATIVE MATERIALS Clothes don't need to be housed in a closet. Instead, hang them on a clothes rod, using colorful paper shopping bags for underwear, T-shirts, and sweatshirts.

DISPLAY YOUR WARES Don't keep your beauties behind closed doors. Mix open and closed shelving, and put your Sunday best on display.

accessories

As the architect Mies van der Rohe once said, "God is in the details." This insight reflects one of the pillars of interior style on a budget: make the most of accessories. On one hand, they are a home's personal signature—a visual diary of who you are and what you love. On the other, they are the practical objects that you couldn't live without.

Accessories usually fall into two camps: functional items such as dishes, flatware, coffeepots, and vases, and objects that are intended purely for decoration, such as a child's finger-painting, a pristine shell found on a beach, or a dried posy of red roses from a former lover.

Functional doesn't have to mean boring. The trick is to combine chic looks with usefulness. If you are buying brandnew flatware, for example, chain stores often have solid stainless-steel sets at reasonable prices. Find a set that the store intends to keep in stock, and spread the cost by buying a few pieces every week. Most stores stock cheap-'n'-cheerful plastic flatware sets, which are perfect garnish for Pop-style interiors. For the real thing— silverware—you can snap up a bargain by ferreting for heirloom sets or buying individual pieces, such as bone-handled knives, from secondhand markets, antique sales, and secondhand stores.

THIS PICTURE Accessories do not have to match. Moroccan tea glasses, secondhand china, used cookie tins, and plastic glasses mix like old friends socializing at a party. Cluster items together this way, but don't clutter. Give everything room to breathe.

OPPOSITE, TOP Cheerful candy-colored plastic cups and a pea-green lemon squeezer are just part of a set of mismatched objects that introduce color, funk, and form to this display.

OPPOSITE, MIDDLE An enamel milk jug makes a convenient teaspoon holder. Plastic-handled flatware sets, available from most chain stores, make an economical alternative to traditional silverware.

OPPOSITE, BOTTOM Accessorize your sink with cheap-'n'-cheerful utensils; don't hide them behind cupboard doors. Put them in easy-to-reach locations, just like these plastic fantastics, which have been hung from hooks in an apparently casual way.

When looking for functional objects at bargain prices, think about which culture has a penchant for a particular pastime—the Far East's passion for tea-drinking, for example. A trip to your local Chinatown will reveal hand-painted teapots, glazed bowls, and dainty cups. For delicate tea glasses, elegant silver teapots, and low-priced earthenware with colorful glazes in cumin yellow, aqua blue, and russet red, try Middle Eastern stores.

Funky functional objects can easily be made to double as decoration—all they need is a showcase. For example, when it comes to china and teapots, you don't always have to choose plates that match. Instead, pick a color, an era (1950s), or a pattern (geometrics); then track appropriate pieces down, creating a covetable collection to display on kitchen wall-racks or shelves.

Accessories are also about pure decoration. Objects express not only your tastes, but also your wit, passions, and past. Sometimes they are simple mementos: a seashell from a midwinter trip to the beach. Or they may be funny—a collection of kitsch fridge

OPPOSITE, MAIN PICTURE **Look out for packaging with panache. Storage has endless accessory possibilities, as this tea caddy shows. You can find containers like these in your local Chinatown.**
OPPOSITE, INSET **These butter-yellow teacups make the viewer do a double-take. Transformed into a bright pair of spring bulb containers, they show how a little ingenuity goes a long way when it comes to style.**
ABOVE, FAR LEFT **Strings of bejeweled necklaces stored on hooks in this bedroom glamorize a white tongue-and-groove wall.**
ABOVE LEFT **Some accessories can be grown. Many of the best frills are provided by Mother Nature.**
ABOVE **For elegant silver teapots and colorful teaglasses, head for your local Middle Eastern store. Apart from tea sets, you will also find inexpensive ceramics, such as tagines and Moorish serving dishes.**

LEFT Why leave on display
an unsightly household item
such as a bottle of dishwasher
detergent when you can hide it
in a French-style milk jar? Use
accessories, especially storage
containers, to house kitchen
bits and pieces. Chipped mugs,
soft-drink cans, vases, sugar
bowls—anything will do.

RIGHT Disguise and decorate.
A pair of red kitchen gloves
hangs over a stainless-steel
pail, which conceals household
cleaners. The owner has used a
practical solution to add visual
interest. Cleaning takes on the
feel of an elegant activity rather
than an onerous chore.

FAR RIGHT Instead of spending
a lot of money on a regular
supply of fresh flowers,
accessorize your vases with
permanent decorations. Dried
grasses and flowers, wands
and windmills, bring a twist
of long-lasting color.

INSET Use open shelving to
display much loved pieces
such as these covetable mugs
collected on a trip to New York.

top tips
for accessories

CHOOSE PIECES WITH FORM AND FUNCTION
When buying functional objects, either choose investment pieces and try to spread the cost or look for good secondhand objects and stylish plastic replicas.

ABANDON THE URGE TO MATCH Instead of buying six brand-new champagne glasses, think *Breakfast at Tiffany's* and trawl secondhand stores for individual bowl-shaped glasses.

PUT FUNCTIONAL OBJECTS ON DISPLAY Hang kitchen utensils from butcher's hooks; showcase pretty teacups; leave jars of dried fruit on benches.

ACCESSORIZE, DON'T CLUTTER Place objects where they create visual surprises. One beautiful item on a shelf says more than a whole army of pieces.

ADORN YOUR HOME WITH FLOWERS Bring color, scent, and vitality indoors with bunches and sprays of unusual and everyday flowers.

MAKE YOUR HOME A PERSONAL DIARY Decorate with things that you have collected over the years: old postcards, an alabaster cat from a vacation in Egypt, old family portraits.

ABOVE **Examples of old technologies, such as this 1930s Bakelite telephone, are one way to instil a sense of individuality and character in your home.**
LEFT **Old fruit-stewing jars have become kitchen storage containers. Seeds, legumes, nuts, pastas, and other foods make eye-catching decoration, particularly when housed in sculptural transparent containers. A kitchen without food on display looks famished, so use food as an accessory.**

magnets from around the globe. And, sometimes pieces come with their own personal history—heirloom vases, for example. All sorts of things with great intrinsic worth cost next to nothing.

Items such as sculptural vases, old perfume bottles, and French milk pitchers can be real showstoppers. All they need is a pedestal or a shelf canvas. As interiors author Julie Iovine recommends, "The secret of good display is to go to the extreme. Miscellaneous objects placed on a table or shelves tend to disappear. Try grouping together objects that are all of one color or material, or set one piece with an interesting shape in splendid isolation."

Finally, don't forget nature, which comes free in the form of driftwood, pebbles, dried grasses, and so on. Hand-picked, they can revitalize a space in an instant. Instead of conventional displays, go for big seed pods, single-stem exotic flowers, or one huge vase of tulips. Plants take a small investment. Buy them young and nurture—all it takes is water, light, and a bit of love.

THIS PICTURE Pillows are indispensable in any chic living space. On a practical level, they provide comfort, but as an accessory they inject color and personality. And you can change them on a whim. Instead of buying a new shirt this season, try on a pillow instead.
LEFT A pair of unsightly radiators, which occupy a lot of wall space, have become canvases for unusual wall-hangings: dishtowels decorated with plumbing motifs.
BELOW LEFT An interior's personal signature is found in the details. Some, including the wide-framed picture of a child's footprint, are purely for decoration.

HTIW

lighting

When it comes to adding chic, lighting does so much for so little, and offers many different options. Within the three categories of home illumination—general lighting, task lighting and feature lighting—there are six main tools: uplighting, downlighting, wall washing, feature lighting, color, and controls.

With general lighting, you can use any or all of the six tools to add a sense of space to your home. Lights, like color, have the power to make a room seem bigger or smaller. For example, a soft wash from a wall sconce makes walls appear wider and larger. Downlights dotted around the edges of a ceiling can also make a small room seem more spacious.

Other ways of maximizing general light are inexpensive. Employ optical illusion by marrying mirrors with light, for example. In a bathroom, a mirror with striplights on each side will bounce light around the room. Transparent glass wall dividers and pale color schemes also maximize light and, with it, space.

Task lighting puts practicalities first. Its purpose is to make sure you can see what you are doing— a must when it comes to kitchen counters or bathroom mirrors. For reading lamps and desk lights, choose portable options, which you can

ABOVE **Use a metal lampshade for a utilitarian feel or buy a standard lamp and spray it in a color to suit your room.**
ABOVE LEFT **Trawl your local Chinatown in search of candy-colored paper shades like this one. Japanese rice-paper shades, which come in contemporary shapes, are wonderfully kind to wallets.**
LEFT **One alternative is to reclaim and recycle. An old storm lantern, given a loving lick of red paint, lights up the life of this apartment.**
OPPOSITE **Attaching a chain-store light to a wire provides spot illumination in this child's bedroom. There is no need for bank-busting electrical work.**

A wide variety of illumination allows you to light up your life while keeping your bank balance in the black.

THIS PICTURE **All good lighting schemes, particularly in the kitchen, need to include adequate task lighting. Here a utility lamp has been hung beside a storage rack for kitchen utensils.**

ABOVE RIGHT **Normally a gooseneck lamp such as this French antique would be office-bound, but in this Dutch apartment it creates great task lighting for a chef.**

MIDDLE RIGHT **Wall sconces offer space-saving ways to create washes of light over walls. This plastic version adds form to a naked wall.**

RIGHT **A basic outdoor wall light has been mounted on a ceiling.**

THIS PICTURE **Mini lights give a soft, playful feel to this hard-edged interior. Strings of this type are perfect for creating coils of light in corners or garlands of light in stairwells or along hallways. Here, skeleton leaves bought from a florist are wrapped around the base of each tiny light.**

INSET **Make your own shade. Here a simple bulb has been given a makeover with a sculptural wire frame. You can go a step farther and create your own light concoction with a cover of vintage fabrics or playful papers.**

LEFT A secondhand chandelier with delicately sculpted bulbs adds glitz and glamour to this living room. Find cheap reproductions or source secondhand.
BELOW LEFT AND FAR LEFT An eye-catching Chinese lightshade injects a twist of the exotic, and strands of driftwood make an equally elegant lightshade display.

move from room to room as needed. Hallways, stairways, and passageways need to be well lit. A cheap solution is to run a string of mini tree lights the length of the corridor or use lengths of "rope" lights—a run of small "pea" bulbs set into a flexible rubber covering. These snakelike illuminations have a lamp life of 10,000 hours—approximately five years of normal use.

Feature lighting is precisely directed lighting that is used to draw the eye to a beautiful piece. Lighting can be a feature in itself, of course. A single distinctive floorlight, such as a secondhand Castiglioni "Swan" lamp, adds grace and glamour. A secondhand chandelier, lit with candles, can be equally alluring.

A little inventiveness goes a long way: for funky shades, wrap 1950s fabrics around old lampshades or dot rows of different color lightbulbs down hallways. Or think dual purpose: Tom Dixon's "Jack" light doubles as a stool, for example. Choosing the right lightbulb for your needs also makes an enormous difference to a light's effectiveness.

Last, begin with the end in mind. Whether you are choosing general, task, or feature lighting, plan your lighting scheme thoroughly from the outset. Putting right mistakes caused by bad planning is often the most costly exercise of all.

top tips for lighting

ENJOY NATURAL LIGHT Make the most of sunlight, moonlight, and firelight. All cast a beautiful glow and bring softness and warmth into a room.

INSTALL DIMMER SWITCHES Nothing changes a room as quickly as brightening or dimming the light source. Create intimate moods in an instant.

BE INNOVATIVE String up a row of Chinese lanterns; use Christmas tree lights at all times of the year; dot candles in antique storm lanterns around a room; invent your own shades.

LIGHT UP YOUR LIFE WITH THE RIGHT BULB Halogen bulbs are flattering for faces and provide directional light, while incandescent bulbs cast a reddish glow and are the choice for everyday use.

ECONOMIZE ON BULBS Compact fluorescent lamps (CFLs or striplights) use one quarter of the electricity used by a standard incandescent lightbulb and last up to 13 times longer.

materials

Hard materials such as wood and stone come in all shapes, sizes, and prices. Before deciding where to spend money, consider these questions. How long are you likely to stay in your home? Are you renovating a property for resale? Or are you improving a rental property?

Start by writing down your needs and then plan how to get the most from your budget. Think about where you would like to spend money, but don't forget areas that need special investment. For example, whether you are staying or selling, areas of heavy wear-and-tear such as entranceways—which give visitors or prospective buyers their first impressions—need to look good. It is worth stretching your budget for floor coverings that have both beauty and longevity, such as wood, stone, and high-quality wool carpets.

When it comes to traditional materials, there are ways to achieve handsome looks for less. If you're lucky, you may find an original wooden floor hiding under a carpet, or a trip to an architectural salvage yard may yield secondhand wooden floors at bargain prices. Alternatives include less expensive softwoods such as pine, even cheaper chipboards and hardboards, or veneers. Veneers have wood's good looks at a fraction of the price of the real thing, but a veneer floor may need to be replaced once every five years.

ABOVE **A mirror-fronted medicine cabinet has been covered with colorful refrigerator magnets.**
ABOVE RIGHT **This cast-iron radiator has a robust look and feel. Think about the image that materials convey when choosing furniture and fixtures.**
BELOW RIGHT **Many older homes have interesting features such as this rustic door. Live in a home for a while before starting to redesign and redecorate, so you can decide what you really want to keep and what you want to lose. Peel back fusty carpets and scrape off old wallpaper to see what materials lie beneath.**
OPPOSITE **Sleek stainless-steel office drawers add hi-tech utility chic to an Amsterdam apartment.**

Make the most of materials at little cost by combining and contrasting. Mix rough with smooth, dark with light, and old with new.

THIS PICTURE AND INSET
Sliding corrugated plastic doors and glass bricks allow light to filter through, keeping a sense of airiness and light. Don't ignore industrial-style building materials such as these, which make inexpensive alternatives to domestic building materials. Buy from any good building supplier.
OPPOSITE, ABOVE LEFT **An oval corrugated-glass panel makes an eye-catching cabinet door. Textured glass allows the viewer to recognize shapes and forms without being able to discern detail.**
OPPOSITE, BELOW LEFT **Create your own kitchen cabinets from medium-density or high-density fiberboard. There are all sorts of ways to customize cupboard doors. In this kitchen, the doors are painted in various shades of blue and contrasted with cut-out holes in place of handles.**

Stone floor coverings—granite, limestone, sandstone, and marble—are generally expensive. Unless you buy these materials from architectural salvage yards or discover flagstones lurking beneath an overlaid floor, it is, economically speaking, better to buy imitations. Concrete or machine-made colored tiles, for example, cost less, are almost equally durable, and come in neutral colors. Lower down the price ladder, linoleums and vinyls are now available in stonelike patterns. While some of these covers won't last as long as the real thing, they make attractive lookalikes.

In the early 17th century, glass was the preserve of the wealthy. While it is still a relatively expensive material, it is the most effective way of bringing more light and space into your home. There are alternatives, however. If you want glass with effects—such as etched or sand-blasted glass—you don't need to spend a fortune. For example, you can use rice paper or gauze covers to create the same feel as sand-blasted glass. Glass's cheaper cousin is plastic, which

THIS PICTURE **A wall of uneven handmade white tiles from Portugal introduces a beautiful human touch to this apartment in Amsterdam.**
INSET **Use materials to create a style. Sleek and shiny light woods, such as those used to construct this kitchen bench and shelf, project an image that is clean and modernist—while rough, weather-worn hardwoods add a rustic feel to an interior.**
OPPOSITE, ABOVE LEFT **Fake it. Instead of spending the earth on expensive materials, find convincing lookalikes such as this veneered wooden kitchen cabinet with transparent sliding doors.**
OPPOSITE, BELOW, LEFT TO RIGHT **A laminated countertop looks chic but costs much less than the alternatives; steel handles give a streamlined look to simple white kitchen cabinets; this galvanized-steel bucket illustrates how materials can become features in their own right.**

top tips for materials

PLAN YOUR BUDGET For high-traffic areas such as hallways, spend money on good materials. If you buy too cheaply, you are likely to have to buy twice.

CUT CORNERS AND COSTS Consider alternatives to wood, stone, metal, glass, tiles, and plaster. Synthetics such as vinyl, plastics, and veneers often have similar looks for half the price.

BE OPEN-MINDED If you know the color and feel you want, try a cheap option. Substitute chocolate-brown cork tiles for parquet floors, and opaque plastic curtains for glass screens, for example.

GO FOR NEARLY NEW Make the most of existing architectural details or scour architectural salvage yards, junk yards, and dumpsters.

INVEST FOR THE FUTURE If you are planning to sell your property in the near future, invest most in the materials in the kitchen and bathroom, the two rooms that most influence purchasers.

LEFT Paint peeling off an old plaster wall adds a bohemian feel for no cost at all.
OPPOSITE, CLOCKWISE FROM ABOVE LEFT A former railroad tie makes a beautiful mantel shelf; this study in a London warehouse conversion contrasts graphic wallpaper with white-painted tiles; panels of wood have been painted white to create texture in a contemporary fireplace surround; exposed brick, stainless steel, and tiles show how an eclectic combination of natural materials can be brought together in a perfectly natural way.

does the work much more cheaply in many places, such as bathroom screens and room dividers.

Metals such as stainless steel, copper, and wrought iron are also reasonably expensive, but they make good investments. Although stainless-steel surfaces in the kitchen require an initial outlay, these look good year after year. Other ways to employ metals are to reuse and recycle. Harness metal's different looks—shiny, rusty, sleek, or raw—and use them to advantage. Old wrought-iron bedsteads from scrapyards and antique shops make romantic headboards and footboards for basic beds, while scaffold poles can be turned into industrial-style curtain rods.

Last but certainly not least among materials are ceramics, which encompass an array of products. Secondhand ceramics can introduce color and pattern to your home at little cost. Whether you are using floor tiles, old ceramic sinks, or broken mosaic wall coverings, ceramics are incredibly versatile and durable. In bathrooms, tile floors and walls create cheap, hard-wearing surfaces, and white ceramic sanitaryware is smooth to the touch, sculptural—and affordable; in kitchens, tiles make hygienic easy-to-clean backsplashes.

flooring

Don't let flooring absorb your entire budget. Even if you have more panache than cash, there is a good choice of low-cost floors that look and feel fabulous. Woods—both hardwoods and softwoods—are regular chart-toppers.

Hardwoods such as mahogany, teak, oak, ash, and maple are generally darker and more expensive than softwoods. Architectural salvage yards and construction sites are the best places to find them at affordable prices. Softwoods such as pine and cedar come in lighter shades and are cheaper—but even better value (and just as chic) are plywood and chipboard floors, made from various kinds of softwood bound with resin. For a wood feel for even less, choose veneers from home stores.

Wood feels warm underfoot, but does not provide the same quality of comfort as carpets and rugs. Research has shown the wisdom of investing in a carpet with a wool content of at least 80 percent. These 80/20 wool-and-manmade-fiber mixes strike a balance between comfort, color retention, and wear. For extra comfort or to minimize wear-and-tear in high-traffic areas, rugs provide a quick, cheap solution. Alternatives to more expensive conventional wool or Persian-style rugs are Indian cotton dhurries, tatami mats, fleece rugs, and skins.

THIS PICTURE AND INSETS **As this trio of pictures illustrates, wood—a budget-style staple—comes in many guises. Hardwoods (inset below) are dark, hard-wearing, and handsome but costlier than softwoods (inset above). Unless you have an old hardwood floor that can be restored, scour salvage yards for reclaimed floors. To achieve a wood look for less, opt for plywood (this picture).** OPPOSITE, RIGHT **Terracotta brick-like tiles, popular in Mediterranean countries, are cool underfoot but fabulously hard-wearing. Good for kitchens, bathrooms, hallways, and other heavily used areas, these tiles come from the school of hard knocks, keeping their looks through many splashes and crashes.**

THIS PICTURE **Hexagonal white ceramic tiles make an elegant, waterproof bathroom surface. Cheap, effective bathroom surfaces include non-porous ceramic tiles, durable rubber tiles, and swathes of linoleum. Unless the bathroom is for adults only, avoid wood (which warps) and carpet and rush matting (both of which rot).**
INSET, RIGHT **A slate-gray sisal cover provides a durable foot-friendly surface for these stairs.**

THIS PICTURE **Concrete paving tiles have been used to make a solid, durable floor in a London kitchen. Varnished to resemble quarry tiles, they offer a neutral backdrop to everyday living.**
INSET, RIGHT **Square terracotta tiles form the foundation of a grand entrance. If you lay such tiles yourself, make sure the grouting is smooth and even—or the floor will require elbow grease to keep clean.**

RIGHT **Terracotta tiles with white grouting make a warm Mediterranean backdrop for a modern interior. Apart from walls, floors are the largest visual backdrops in your home. Avoid expensive mistakes by choosing floors that fit in with the overall color scheme.**

For spaces that need extra-durable flooring, there is nothing to beat poured concrete or concrete tiles.

THIS PICTURE Glorious paint transforms this humdrum staircase into a striking feature. All you need is a wood primer, two layers of undercoat, and a top coat. An area such as this requires up to five coats of varnish. Choose high-gloss for a shiny, easy-care finish.

ABOVE RIGHT Royal-blue rubber adds a regal touch to a set of wooden stairs. Hard-wearing and non-slip, rubber is ideal for heavy-traffic areas.

RIGHT AND FAR RIGHT Wood and other hard floors are often noisy when walked on. Apart from soaking up sound, rugs, mats, and dhurries are a cheap and chic way of introducing color, texture, and warmth. The white-painted floor in the picture on the far right has been softened by the addition of a knitted wool rug.

Natural-fiber flooring—think sisal, coir, jute, abaca, and grass—is ideal if you are decorating your home on a shoestring. Use coverings made from natural fibers for entire floors or as mats and runners. Jute is the softest of these and looks like silk (perfect for bedrooms), but it is not as hardwearing as sisal, which is strong but supple (perfect for hallways and bathrooms).

The latest byword in chic is sheet flooring. Lino—as linoleum is sometimes known—with its bold and striking patterns, came into vogue in the 1920s, during the Bauhaus period. Made of flax and oil, lino has shed its dull fusty image and re-emerged as a desirable retro material. Vinyl, lino's PVC rival, has now become just as chic. Strike out with a stunning style, such as a vinyl floor embedded with photographic images of whatever you like.

Another unsung budget-style hero is rubber flooring. Like lino and vinyl, rubber is waterproof and practical, but it also tends to be warmer, quieter, and softer to the touch. Alternatively, cork, made from bark bonded with polyurethane resin, has the visual good looks of wood, but is inexpensive. It can also be painted.

For spaces that need extremely durable flooring, nothing beats poured concrete—ask your local builder to quote a price for laying a concrete floor. Stone is generally expensive, but you can find beautiful tiles that will give you the same looks for less. Tiles, too, are able to withstand countless foot treads and are available in a huge choice of colors.

Shop around for flooring. If you want to save money, don't jump on the first floor you see.

top tips for flooring

BUY THE RIGHT FLOOR FOR THE RIGHT SPACE Floors in kitchens and bathrooms need to be durable, water-resistant, hygienic, and easy to clean—invest in linoleum, rubber flooring, concrete, tiles, or wood.

USE HEAVY-DUTY FLOORING FOR HIGH-TRAFFIC AREAS If you have a lino floor in the kitchen, for example, put down an extra cover such as a strip of tiles or a sisal mat in front of the sink.

PAINT WOODEN, HARDBOARD, OR CHIPBOARD FLOORS Working out to the door, apply a wood primer, followed by two coats of undercoat and a top coat. Finish with three coats of varnish (or five in areas of heavy traffic).

USE WHAT YOU ALREADY HAVE If you have moved into an older home, you may find an original wooden floor right under your nose. Strip back old carpets to see what lies beneath.

GET LUXURY FOR LESS If you yearn for the dark browns of old wood, consider using cork tiles instead. If you want a shag-pile carpet, buy the next best thing: a luxuriously thick fleece rug (available from chain stores).

the spaces

relaxing

LEFT AND FAR LEFT A successfully organized living area has plenty of storage for the things that give you pleasure. To accommodate your pastimes, make the most of every space, as this homeowner has done, by creating shelving on walls and stacking books in an alcove that is too small for any other purpose.
BELOW Former apple crates nailed to a wall create a stylish, boxy set of shelves.
OPPOSITE A generously large beige modular sofa creates a useful division between the sitting and dining areas. At the end of the sofa, a space-saving nest of tables is ideal for everyday use, as well as providing surfaces for display.

A daybed in a sunlit conservatory ... a luxuriously large black leather sofa parked against a soft pink wall ... a playroom by day, a home cinema by night. Spaces to relax now come in many shapes and forms. "Living rooms" are multi-functional spaces where we unwind, watch television, play games, socialize, entertain, surf the internet, work—the list goes on and on.

If you want to design and decorate a living room for less, start by thinking carefully about what the room will be used for. While most living rooms are earmarked to accommodate a sofa and chairs, everyone's needs need to be taken into account. Will this room be primarily a place to sprawl and read? Will it be a playground and entertainment center for rowdy children? Will you end up eating supper there? Will you use it for work? Write down the answers to these questions, asking everyone who lives with you to contribute.

Location, location, location is the first thing to consider. In some cases, architectural solutions can make a big difference. Knocking down walls to create all-in-one spaces, conservatory extensions, and attic conversions don't have to be prohibitively expensive as long as you can find an architect who appreciates the meaning of "low budget." Or a room swap may be in order—if, for example, the master bedroom is the most spacious room in the house and

has sun-catching bays and an unused fireplace. When you have decided where to site the living room, your next tasks are to take measurements and go out shopping.

For the room's canvases—its floors and walls—use color and texture to maximize space and instill a mood. You know the rules: pale colors make walls appear farther apart, while dark colors make them seem closer.

Create an easygoing backdrop to daily life by choosing neutral paint or wallpaper or pale wood paneling. Alternatively, you could harness the emotional associations of color to define the room's purpose: yellow and orange are conversation stimulants; blues and purples designate calm; red is perfect for an environment devoted to eating and entertaining.

ABOVE **The diva of this living room is an antique travel trunk, which doubles as a coffee table. Draped elegantly over the sofas, dust covers and old blankets make the perfect throws, softening the room's lines.** RIGHT **Forgo the traditional three-piece set and reclaim distinctive pieces. A black-painted wooden fisherman's chest stands in front of a metal Detroit gilder bench, a former 1960s porch favorite, while to the right is a 1930s leather club chair.**

RIGHT AND BELOW RIGHT The hearth was traditionally the heart of the home. Even in rooms where the hearth is no longer used for a fire, the eye is always drawn toward it. Instead of concealing an unused fireplace, use the alcove to display objects of visual interest such as those illustrated here—an autumnal display of gourds and twisted branches, and a row of retro paper bags that double as magazine racks.

THIS PICTURE **A vintage Venetian chandelier makes a glamorous centerpiece in this light, airy living room. Leaving the room free of curtains and painting its walls and floors white is a simple way to create a feeling of incredible spaciousness. Optical illusions can reduce your building bills: why knock down a wall when a coat of light-colored paint produces the same result?**

At the end of a long day's work, there is nothing more satisfying than kicking off your shoes. The kindest underfoot solution for weary feet is a carpet or rug. Indian dhurries, secondhand Persian carpets, and chain-store weaves are gentle on the purse as well as the feet, but have the advantage of introducing softness, style, and color. Other low-cost solutions include rugs made from secondhand carpets with the edges turned over or bound, sheepskins, or soft natural fibers such as jute.

The next big element to consider is furnishings. If you plan to do a lot of entertaining, you need furniture that is flexible and easy to move, perhaps arranged around a central focus such as a fireplace or a coffee table. If the living room doubles as a work room, you may want to think about installing a fold-away table that can be hidden in a cabinet in the evenings when it is no longer needed.

Create an easygoing backdrop with neutral paint or wallpaper or pale wood paneling.

ABOVE RIGHT **A Biedermeier bateau-style sofa provides seating for several people, while a wooden folding chair easily opens up to create another place to rest. For chic seating, reclaim outdoor furniture and bring it indoors. White household candles in candelabra add style. The floor light is homemade from a floor lamp attached to a stand.**
RIGHT AND FAR RIGHT **You can use a stove to heat a room, as this homeowner has. The former fireplace has contemporary good looks, right down to its smooth modern mantelpiece lined with *objets d'art*.**

Chain stores have a good selection of adaptable armchairs and sofas—particularly if you want a fold-out spare bed—at reasonable prices.

To give mass-produced pieces of furniture a more individual character, simply sew your own slipcovers out of vintage fabrics or dress them with throws bought from secondhand stores; or use old scarves, plaid blankets, an assortment of colorful cushions, cast-off bedspreads, or ethnic fabrics such as Indonesian batiks or Indian saris. Rescue and revive antique leather sofas, which

ABOVE **Neutral colors such as gray, taupe, and beige contrast with vibrant dandelion yellows, fresh greens, and highlights of red to create an inspirational living space. Fabrics, including the soft sheepskins and colored rugs, add texture. The sliding door, painted in bold blocks of color, is made from reclaimed wood.**

THIS PICTURE For family living areas, use movable furniture to accommodate everyone's needs. If you move, you can always take it with you. A television on castors is easily tucked away, while the red pouf is extra seating or a foot rest. **RIGHT AND INSET** Create visual interest at next to no expense. Instead of papering your entire room, cover a single wall with vintage paper, as the owner of this Amsterdam home has done. Here a large pine storage chest doubles as a daybed. For stylish art on a budget, ask a budding Leonardo to draw you a picture.

OPPOSITE **This tucked-away living area in a guest cottage makes the most of the space available. From the chinoiserie lampshade to the pale blue coffee table, the look is light, fresh, and contemporary. The vertical lines of the white tongue-and-groove walls and the horizontal lines on the ceiling make the room appear larger than it is.**

RIGHT **Dress your couch in a little reversible number. Striped canvas meets exotic floral in this example of a pillow cover sewn from recycled fabrics.**

FAR RIGHT **Instead of buying cut flowers, grow plants from bulbs or seeds and just add water.**

BELOW **Garden-plucked red roses displayed in a former vinegar bottle cost nothing but add much.**

BELOW RIGHT **Make your own sofa. Transform an old bed into a laidback sofa with a colorful canvas cover. Adorn it with an entourage of pillows and cushions in different shapes and sizes.**

last a lifetime, from secondhand stores, garage sales, and salvage yards. Other options for stylish seating including chaises longues, slouchy armchairs, garden seats, wicker chairs, old church pews, and antique leather club chairs. For contemporary retro looks, chic alternatives include colorful beanbags, low-slung plastic seats, and inflatable blow-up sofas and armchairs softened with 1960s-style cushions.

For low-cost, contemporary-looking storage, choose an inexpensive modular system of the type that can be found in most large furniture warehouses. Flat-packed shelves and units are also kind to your budget and can easily be given a facelift with a coat of paint. Among other resurrected storage options are old armoires, 1960s sideboards, simple ottomans, chests, and trunks. For smaller storage for videos and CDs, try former hat boxes, shoeboxes, and wooden wine boxes.

Don't forget that relaxing areas are often public spaces where you are likely to entertain visitors. They are ideal settings in which to showcase the things you love and objects that have special meaning for you—such items may provide conversational starting points. Fresh flowers always make a room welcoming.

Efficient lighting costs little but adds much. During the day, maximize natural daylight by extending windows and adding skylights. During the evening, use a combination of lighting solutions such as floor lamps, wall lights, and reading lights. Create a sense of theater. The living room is, after all, a backdrop for life.

ABOVE **An eclectic combination of covers—from zebra stripes and blue velvet to eyelet lace and chinoiserie—make the ingredients of a pillow party on this stylish sofa. Among the wall decorations is a stencil of a moose head beside favorite photographs.**
RIGHT **A hot-pink artificial flowerhead broken up into petals and threaded onto a piece of blue string creates a low-cost, high-impact garland.**
OPPOSITE, ABOVE **A plain white couch cover dyed a bright aqua blue is the focal point of this light and airy living room. Old intact sofa covers have no sell-by date—all they need, as here, is a darker dye.**
OPPOSITE, BELOW **A sheer voile curtain diffuses the light in this living room, giving the whole space an ethereal quality. With such a translucent backdrop, the floor, coated in thick glossy paint, also reflects the light. A grand display of flowers on the table adds color, glamour, scent, and chic.**

top tips for relaxing

FASHION A STYLE Reinvent a look or create your own style and accessorize. For example, think faded grandeur (peeling paint effects, gilt frames), modern natural (leather sofas, voile curtains) or new retro (inflatable sofas, plastic chairs, vintage geometric cushions).

BE INVENTIVE WITH LIGHTING If your living room has a pendant light, put it on a dimmer switch, replace it with a gothic-style candelabrum lit by candles, or install an unlit feature such as a glittery secondhand chandelier.

USE FABRICS FOR COMFORT Add a splash of color with curtains sewn from old scarves, make pillow covers from old sweaters, reupholster sofas, or dress the floor with a Mexican rug.

MAKE MONEY If you have cash to invest, buy 20th-century collectibles. An Eames lounger bought five years ago has almost trebled in value since. Trawl secondhand stores for pieces by designers such as Robin Day, Verner Panton, Arne Jacobsen, and Philippe Starck.

REVAMP THE HEARTH If you have an empty fireplace, restore it with a secondhand insert and surround. For the same effect without the cost, put a mixture of large church candles and small votives in the fireplace.

cooking and eating

Cooking and eating: two essential, pleasurable activities that can be accommodated both cheaply and chicly. Traditionally, in better off households, these spaces were almost always separated—but, as informality has replaced protocol, stiff-upper-lipped dining rooms have generally come to be regarded as dinosaurs. Modern life has married cooking and eating spaces into one—ideally, large—room.

What kind of arrangement you choose for preparing and eating meals in your home depends on your lifestyle and the people you live with. If you eat out a lot, a well-organized galley kitchen with breakfast bar, stools, a compact refrigerator, and microwave may be enough to satisfy your needs. For people who share their home with family or friends, an area that can accommodate both cooking and dining is the perfect place to catch up at the beginning and end of the day. To create such an area, you may need to knock down a wall between the kitchen and a living room, dining room, or hallway. Architectural changes can be expensive, but, in this case, introducing extra light and space and creating fluidity between rooms is worth its weight in gourmet meals.

ABOVE AND OPPOSITE A wall of white Portuguese tiles visually marks out the kitchen area in this one-room living space. The freestanding unit swallowed most of the budget, but it will last for years.
ABOVE CENTER Old bottles with colored glass or curvaceous shapes make good vases.
ABOVE LEFT Post office sorting shelves have been given a new purpose as kitchen storage. Open shelving of this type costs much less than a built-in kitchen.
BELOW A dark veneer has been added to the doors of this kitchen to give it a 1970s look in keeping with the rest of the building.

Minimalist, retro chic, and farmhouse looks are the best value.

ABOVE The centerpiece of this table is a wine cooler that has been transformed into a stylish vase. The owner made his own table out of plywood. He also built the floor-to-ceiling cupboard, which provides oodles of seamless storage space.

LEFT Custommade plywood doors have been installed to separate a kitchen from a dining area in this small apartment.

OPPOSITE, ABOVE Customize secondhand kitchenware in a color that suits your appetite. Use car spray or enamel paint.

OPPOSITE, BELOW Minimal shelves add horizontal stripes of color to a white wall. Open shelving of this kind gives you the opportunity to keep all your kitchen essentials on display as well as making them easily accessible.

the spaces

RIGHT **The frame around an extractor fan becomes a structural feature in this kitchen when an array of utensils are hung from it.**

FAR RIGHT **Holes in cabinet doors are a cheaper alternative to handles.**

OPPOSITE **Everything in this kitchen can be found in chain stores. The owner has imaginatively exploited all the available space, with tall cabinets reaching up to the ceiling. Chic accessories include a Dualit toaster— an investment buy that comes with a guarantee that it will outlive its owner.**

BELOW **The backdrop to this kitchen is a favorite photograph reproduced as wallpaper by a specialized printer. A glossy plywood floor creates a good-value, hard-working kitchen surface. Note how the wall storage reaches right up to the ceiling.**

Start by deciding on your kitchen layout, bearing in mind that most kitchens are based on the tried and tested L-shape or U-shape. Make a list of the appliances and fixtures you would like to include and decide where you are going to put them; then calculate your budget. Once you've made a room plan and done your homework, it is time to grab your largest shopping bag.

Big-box and chain stores have low-cost, off-the-shelf modern kitchen carcasses. To give them personality, simply accessorize. Or you can fashion your own kitchen from low-cost materials. For example, have cupboards built from inexpensive medium-density fiberboard to create a neat, stylish effect. A carpenter will construct a carcass for you, perhaps from composite board of high density, with doors made from the medium-density version, which you can customize with handles and paint. Use laminates for retro countertops and linoleum for flooring; linoleum makes an attractive kitchen feature for more splash and less cash than the alternatives.

LEFT AND INSET Careful planning has kept this eating area inviting. A light color scheme, from the dishes to the chairs, keeps it looking airy, while a vinyl-coated wipeable floral tablecloth adds shots of color—a decorative theme carried through to the laundry room. **BELOW LEFT** Made of composite board, this utilitarian bench stretches the length of the kitchen, making lots of shelf space for essentials. This kind of style is more affordable than built-in cabinets, but looks just as good. Again, glossy white paint creates a light, bright floor; a kitchen area needs at least five good top coats.

The next subject to consider is the style of your fixtures. High-tech lovers: stop! Don't do it. Sleek, sophisticated elements of this style such as shiny stainless steel and smooth granite cost a bomb. Much better for your budget are minimalist, retro chic, and rustic farmhouse looks.

A minimalist effect is dependent on efficient storage, so take this into account when planning, and remember the basics such as a trash can. If you build in lots of drawers and hidden pull-outs, it's easy to make the most of every inch of space. For china and ceramics, choose nothing but white from chain stores.

The modern retro feel combines cheap materials such as painted wood, checked linoleum, and pastel colors. Hunt down pastel-painted wood and Formica freestanding cabinets from the 1950s and 1960s, and retro accessories such as graphically decorated teacups and teapots. It is also worth looking out for pastel-colored and retro refrigerators.

The farmhouse style fits in with the modern trend for dual-purpose spaces. The main requisite of this type of kitchen is its centerpiece, the table: for a rustic feel, choose an old refectory table or a large

THIS PICTURE **A fresh linen tablecloth and a secondhand candelabrum are all it takes to give this kitchen eating area a formal feel. The most striking feature of the room is the large open plate rack, a simple, easy-to-make device for showing off serving dishes and trays. Above the rack, an Indian garland made of tin frames the room.**

pine table and cover it with a flat-weave cloth. An old ceramic sink complete with reclaimed faucets is another essential. Instead of buying high-tech modern kitchen equipment, go for early examples of gadgets such as coffee grinders, glass juicers, nutcrackers, herb cutters, and weighing scales with sets of brass or iron weights. Similarly, sets of old tea strainers, enamel colanders, rolling pins, and aluminum pots and pans are satisfying to use and display.

Whatever you choose, make sure it is classic, since fashion fads are a waste of time and money. When it comes to building, decorating, and preparing your kitchen, it pays to make the most of anything that's free, such as natural light and features. As chef Peter Gordon says, "It's fantastic working in natural light—it makes preparation much easier and more fun." So put countertops or sinks under windows or install skylights.

Lighting essentials include adequate task lighting over countertops and stoves. For all-in-one spaces, you need flexibility. Dimmer switches can be used to change mood, creating a soft glow for eating or a bright light for cooking. For dining, use candles to give a sense of ritual. Dimmer switches, drop lighting, and wall lights also enhance a sense of occasion.

For walls, the solution may be just beneath that horror show of wallpaper. Expose bricks to add to a rustic look. Most kitchen walls need a wipeable waterproof surface. The cheapest option is paint, but veneer works equally well. Instead of expensive stone tiles, decorate a wall with hardwood ply; you need to seal and paint it.

ABOVE **From the yellow-upholstered chairs to the blue shelf in the background, this eating area has been designed as an enjoyable place to be. A secondhand leather sofa provides an area to sit and chat. On the table are handmade placemats cut from colorful felt, while a driftwood lampshade from South Africa hangs over the table.**
ABOVE RIGHT **Paint your refrigerator with black paint, as this owner has done, and use it to write shopping lists and messages—or simply draw your dreams.**
ABOVE FAR RIGHT **Instead of forking out on china, use cheap-'n'-cheerful plastic picnic plates.**
OPPOSITE **Make the most of basics such as these striped dishtowels and chinoiserie thermoses. Think laterally about kitchen furniture. A set of drawers, once earmarked for a bedroom, are equally at home here.**

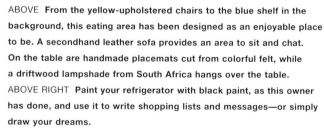

ABOVE **Efficient kitchens have ample storage. Here an unused stairwell has become a kitchen cabinet containing everything but the kitchen sink.**
ABOVE RIGHT **Mix old and new. Keep what you have, but add a modern twist. In this kitchen, above the old gas stove is a smart new extractor fan, and a sleek zinc counter crowns a rough wooden cabinet.**
RIGHT **White china never goes out of style.**
OPPOSITE, ABOVE **Floor-to-ceiling cabinets provide an abundance of storage space in this minimalist kitchen. Again, holes are used instead of handles to give easy access to the contents of drawers and cabinets at next to no cost.**
OPPOSITE, BELOW **The bright and breezy palette of blond wood and white paint in this kitchen maximizes the impression of space.**

Particular areas—stove and sink backsplashes and counters, for example—need durable, hard-working surfaces. Ceramic hard-glazed tiles, used in combination with epoxy grout and water-resistant resin, make low-cost, easy-to-maintain countertops. If you have a little money to invest, marble is the chef's choice.

The most important piece of furniture in any dining area is the table, the bigger the better. While inexpensive tables are available from chain stores, you can always use glass desks or make your own from a smooth door mounted on trestles.

To enjoy long, lingering lunches to the full, your guests will need comfortable seats. For alternative shoestring seating, buy old church pews, use rustic garden furniture seats, old school chairs, or fold-out picnic chairs, or reupholster retro chairs. To soften hard edges, simply fashion cushions to fit.

As for appliances such as ovens and refrigerators, the cheapest option is to buy secondhand. Kitchens are often the last rooms that people selling their homes redesign and redecorate in order to attract buyers—and kitchen appliances may be the first things new owners rip out—so it is not too difficult to find second-hand items of reasonably good quality. Otherwise, look out for lesser-known brands, which sell more cheaply—or compromise: if you eat out a lot, you can probably make do with a microwave rather than an oven.

top tips for cooking and eating

PLAN TO MAKE PERFECT Before you part with a penny, define exactly what you want from your kitchen. In the long run, you'll save yourself time, heartache, and money.

MAKE A NOMADIC DINING ROOM To transform any room into an impromptu dining room, go Eastern. Mount a smooth door on bricks, cover it with a sheet or an ethnic cloth, and strew cushions around it on the floor.

USE BIG IDEAS FOR SMALL SPACES If your cooking and eating area is small, use optical illusion to enlarge it: choose reflective surfaces and glass tables; use a pale color scheme. For extended vistas, hang a mirror above the dining area.

MAKE COUNTERS WORK It's worth spending money on high-quality countertops, which bear the brunt of hard work and are a nuisance to replace. Investment choices include marble, granite, hardwoods, and stainless steel.

PROTECT HARD-WEAR AREAS If you don't have the budget to invest in a good countertop or floor, get the next best thing. Buy marble slabs and thick wooden chopping boards, and put rubber mats in front of sinks.

sleeping

Bedrooms are usually the last rooms to receive our attention when it comes to interior design. Yet sleep is one of the most important things we do. Studies have shown that, for every hour's sleep we forfeit each week, we reduce our IQ by one point. Getting a good night's sleep is vital to both our wellbeing and our intelligence.

Transforming a bedroom into a haven doesn't have to be ruinously expensive. Most bedrooms are simple spaces, where the bed takes center stage. While clothes-aholics might give priority to installing a walk-in closet, most of us accept that our bedroom also needs to serve as our dressing room. To create a restful but hard-working space, the trick is to blend practicalities—such as capacious clothes storage—with aesthetics.

The first thing you must invest in for health's sake is a decent bed. Most sleep experts advise buying a new bed every ten years. If the cost hurts, make it easier to endure by thinking of the money spread over the next decade. A supportive, well-cushioned bed is fundamental to a good night's sleep. Choose "pocket sprung" mattresses (mattresses sprung with individual coils) to give your

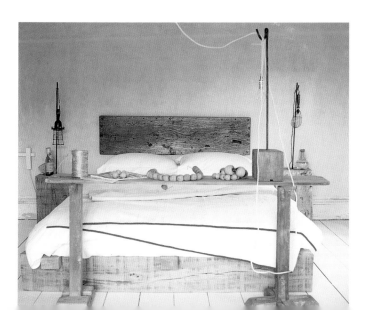

OPPOSITE **A simple racking system creates eye-catching storage for everything from the ironing board to bedside tables. Simple ingenuity has been used to transform an everyday object into a piece of art.**
ABOVE **Puppets, a little girl's dress, and a hot water bottle line up along this picture-perfect plywood rack system.**
ABOVE, INSET **This bed consists of a good-quality mattress mounted on wooden slats, which in turn rest on a base of outdoor building blocks.**
LEFT **A generously sized bed is mounted on old railroad ties, and the weathered-wood theme is carried through to the teak headboard and the bedside tables, made from a block of oak. Flanking the bed are two antique inspection lamps.**

111

ABOVE **Lengths of voile draped over the bed in the style of mosquito nets add an exotic twist to this little girl's room. A paper lampshade provides a crown of color. Bed ends like these often turn up in secondhand stores.**

spine the support it needs. And don't stop at the mattress. Make sure your pillows won't give you nightmares. Invest in the best to make sure your neck and head are adequately supported.

Where you can make savings is on your bed linen and coverings. Pure linen makes a soporific sleeping partner, but it is expensive to buy new. Save yourself wallet-ache by picking up antique or secondhand sheets from flea markets, or sew white linen tablecloths together. A less expensive option, cotton (particularly Egyptian cotton) is soft against naked skin, bought ready-to-use from chain stores.

To dress your bed, buy secondhand wool blankets or stitch together old wool scarves to create a patchwork cover. For decoration, make a collage of old scarves, fabric remnants, picnic blankets, light rugs, and vintage curtains. Instead of a traditional patchwork of tiny squares, choose four big blocks of complementary fabrics.

A comforter is an investment buy. The quality and type of filling in a comforter or duvet affects the price, but you can console your wallet by offsetting the cost with low-priced covers, either bought from chain stores or made by you—all you need is two cotton sheets sewn together and dyed fast in your most-loved color.

To create a tranquil environment, ambience is everything. Keep lighting soft, intimate, and romantic. All you really need is a bedside light. Just buy an old lamp and revamp it with foxy fabrics, or pick a retro classic from a secondhand store. Most bedrooms have a central ceiling light. Dress it for less with a glamorous secondhand chandelier or a Chinese paper lampshade. For instant changes of mood, install a dimmer switch.

ABOVE **Bedrooms often need to double as dressing rooms. Instead of hiding all your gorgeous pieces, put them out on show, making a feature of, for example, a row of shoes.**
LEFT **Fairy lights frame built-in open shelves, which house everything that a little girl needs to keep close at hand.**

THIS PICTURE **Bedrooms need to be soporific spaces. Nothing is kinder to budgets than a pared-back minimalist look, as represented by this attic bedroom painted peaceful white. Apart from the bed, secondhand and vintage books are its only feature, perfectly placed for bedside reading.**
INSET **Bedrooms are fabric magnets. Instead of standard bedding, seek alternatives to sleep with, such as vintage shawls, plaid blankets, antique linens, tablecloths, and saris.**

THIS PICTURE Although it looks like a million dollars, this bedroom was not expensive to put together. Plenty of large soft pillows, pristine white cottons, and a huge body-length mirror add decadent notes. A minimal white shelf makes a stylish floating side table. Instead of putting in a new carpet, the owners have used a big square of carpet with bound edges. When they leave, it can roll up and out the door.

RIGHT **Linen tablecloths bought at a sale make a stylish cover for this bed.**
BELOW **The curtains are made from army tent fabric, which keeps in the warmth and blocks out the light. A shell garland is draped around a wall-mounted bedside light.**
BELOW CENTER **A fabric print has been cut out and nailed to a canvas. To make a similar one, look for bolts of funky graphic fabric.**
BELOW RIGHT **A bedside table can be as simple as this secondhand rustic stool. An old office light makes a perfect reading lamp.**

Bedside tables to put your lights on are another necessity. For a cheap, rustic-style table, sand and varnish an old tree trunk or adapt a coffee table, adding a linen handkerchief to dress it. Upturned crates covered with a paisley silk scarf also make practical side tables at little cost.

When it comes to the all-important business of sleep, windows need to be adequately covered. Darkness helps your body secrete the hormone melatonin, which aids sleep. For total blackout, choose thick fabrics such as denim, canvas, or velvet, and sew blackout material to the side of the curtain facing the window. Shutters bought secondhand and off-the-shelf blinds or shades cut to fit also keep rooms in the dark.

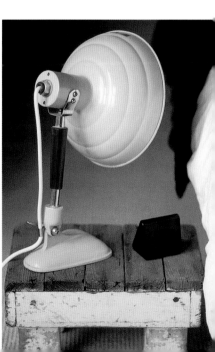

THIS PICTURE **This striped wall was inspired by the colors of a baby jumpsuit (see page 20). Where painting a whole room would be overpowering, painting a single wall can transform the ordinary into the extraordinary. Reclaimed wooden shelving, secondhand cabinets, and a vintage dog-on-wheels are just some of the finds that cost next to nothing. For extra hanging space, hooks have been added to the side of the clothes closet. Its smooth white top is the ideal place for a photo gallery.**

THIS PICTURE **It's smarter to barter. The old doors
in this bedroom were swapped for a bottle of wine.
The unused fireplace alcove, with its exposed brick,
becomes an installation display area.**
INSET **A simple bare wire becomes the perfect place
from which to hang children's clothes. A sheepskin on
the floor adds warmth to bare boards.**

ABOVE Painting the whole fireplace white makes it look like a sculptural relief. White brings with it a sense of peace—the feel of a retreat extends to the accessories, including the chic aromatherapy burner on the mantelpiece.

ABOVE LEFT This fabric-and-wood-framed armoire is an inexpensive and ingenious way to store clothes and shoes without losing a sense of space. Save money on bedroom storage by using every nook and cranny.

LEFT Mix old and new, something plain and something blue. A combination of florals looks soft and pretty.

OPPOSITE An all-white and neutral color scheme pushes the walls out in this serene bedroom. Even the quietly patterned bed linen and pale-colored blanket contribute to the restful palette. To enhance the impression of space, all accessories are strictly white, including the wall-mounted light.

The bedroom is the most important place in the home, but often receives the least attention.

The soles of your feet crave softness and warmth. Investing in a carpet is one option, but a cheaper alternative is to buy a rug to put by the bed. Sheepskin, wool, or silk rugs are the kindest to sleepy feet. For general wallet-friendly flooring, try wood veneers or natural-fiber carpeting such as jute. You'll just need a pair of slippers nearby.

To sleep soundly, perchance to dream, it helps to decorate your bedroom in quiet, calming colors. For color on a budget, you'll need a pot of paint or strips of wallpaper in peaceful patterns and textures. Florals from the 1950s, paisleys, and chinoiserie papers are currently back in vogue: buy vintage papers or reproductions from chain stores.

For mental peace you need your bedroom to be neat and well ordered, which means good storage. Make the most of unused spaces, such as the space under the bed, or create a roomy closet by bringing in the walls with floor-to-ceiling storage, made seamless with push-catch doors.

Clothes need their own home. Again, there's no need to spend a fortune on furniture. A simple open clothes rack and stylish boxes can be used to make low-cost storage. Keep shoes in the boxes they came in, but for display decorate the boxes with retro wallpapers. And don't forget alternative clothes storage such as old office filing cabinets for drawers, stacked tea chests, medicine cabinets, and book shelves.

With such a chic bedroom—put together on a shoestring—you'll be able to hit the pillow at night without taking a hit on your bank account.

ABOVE **This freestanding closet also serves as a headboard. Behind it, open shelves provide storage for pairs of shoes. Rather than hide your beautiful dresses behind closed doors, bring them out to create decorative features. Change the display as often as you change your clothes.**
RIGHT **Instead of a bedside light, use a garland of tree lights woven around metal bed ends.**
OPPOSITE, ABOVE **You don't need a bathroom attached to your master bedroom when you can have a rolltop French-style bateau tub in your boudoir.**
OPPOSITE, BELOW **A bright Asian kite has landed on this bedroom wall, introducing a splash of color. As an alternative to buying bookcases, simply stack books or magazines on top of each other. Adorn walls with anything that catches the eye, from postcards to beads, as illustrated here.**

top tips for sleeping

INVEST IN REST Spend most of your budget on the best bed money can buy. Before buying, lie down on the bed in the showroom for 15 minutes or more, testing different positions for comfort.

ACCESSORIZE FOR LESS Buy good-quality antique-linen sheets or brandnew cotton sheets from chain stores. Adorn your bed with beautiful homemade covers.

RECYCLE, REUSE, AND REINVENT Customize an office filing cabinet and turn it into drawers; store bed linen in an old tea chest; hang a painted broomstick on two long lengths of sturdy string from ceiling hooks and use it as a clothes rod.

GO ZEN One of the most stylish (and cheapest) looks for bedrooms is pure Zen. Clear all surfaces, paint walls a pale color, and choose white and neutral accessories. Stash clothes in a floor-to-ceiling closet.

DRESS SENSE Hang out your glad rags on a rack and color-coordinate, or turn your collection of handbags into art and hang them from wooden clothes pegs spaced evenly along a wall.

bathing

Since its emergence from behind locked doors, the bathroom has received a fundamental makeover. No longer regarded as simply a functional place for washing at the beginning and end of the day, it has become somewhere to relax and luxuriate. But, while designers such as Philippe Starck and Jasper Morrison have given the once-shy bathroom a revamp, the good news is that you don't have to pay designer-label prices to have a chic, sleek home retreat.

When planning a bathroom, go back to basics. Where is the best place in your home for a bathroom? Could you convert a spare bedroom or an attic space? Or does your existing small bathroom have everything, albeit at a squeeze? If the master bedroom is vast, could you sacrifice a corner to create a shower enclosure? Modern shower cubicles can be installed virtually anywhere with the right plumbing—under a staircase or in a hall closet, for example. Save yourself time and money by being clear in your own mind about your priorities.

Next, give a thought to practicalities such as electrical outlets, pipes, plumbing regulations, and ventilation systems—all of which must comply with local regulations. It is crucial to get these details right now, since alterations at a later stage are likely to be costly and disruptive. Regulations vary from area to area, so get advice from a local professional.

Practical considerations aside, it is time to start thinking about how to make your bathroom design "budget friendly." Start with the biggest spaces—the floors and walls. Think about who will use the bathroom. For example, young children love to splash water

ABOVE A picture holdall has acquired a new life as a bathroom laundry bag. The utilitarian metal lightshade complements the sleek and hygienic feel of the room. TOP For inexpensive chic, nothing beats standard sanitaryware such as this sink, which is easy to accessorize. ABOVE RIGHT Matching tiles on bathtub and walls create a seamless, hotellike look.

OPPOSITE **This fiberglass tub is lighter than the traditional cast-iron variety and keeps water warm longer, reducing hot-water bills. If you want your bathtub to double as a shower, save money by buying a plastic shower curtain rather than a glass screen. Concrete plant pots beside the tub make a home for accessories.** BELOW **Bathroom storage needn't be boring—as this former printer's shelf lined with lotions and potions illustrates.**

RIGHT **An awkward alcove has been put to clever use
in this businesslike bathroom. In addition to providing
extra storage space, it has been transformed into a
display cabinet for bathroom essentials such as rolled-
up towels, lotions and potions, and for decorative
items such as framed pictures. The cane basket tucked
away on the bottom shelf is used to conceal less
attractive bathroom items. Underneath the washbasin
is a towel rack, which again makes imaginative use
of otherwise useless space.**

OPPOSITE, BELOW **Built-in storage is an invaluable
asset in a bathroom. One way to accommodate it
is by installing drawers and cabinets in the space
underneath a sink or around a toilet.**

everywhere, so in a bathroom used by children
avoid carpet (which rots) and softwoods (which
warp). Better alternatives are rubber tiles, linoleum,
and non-glazed, non-slip ceramic tiles, which are
hygienic, durable, and water-resistant. For an
adults-only bathroom, the choice widens to include
varnished softwoods, wood veneers, and rubber-
backed, bathroom-quality carpets made from
cotton or synthetic fibers.

Wall coverings must be dampproof and hygienic,
but they can also be used to influence a room's
architecture. For example, if your bathroom is an
odd shape, you can make it look more regular with
a monochrome paint scheme. While white is a
common bathroom choice, it can look reminiscent
of an operating room. Use pastels to introduce
color without reducing the sense of space.
Waterproof paints are the cheapest wall coverings,
but machine-made tiles or yacht-board panels
are also effective, inexpensive coverings. Again,
play architect with visual effects. A long, thin room
looks wider with big square tiles.

ABOVE **A Zenlike feel—where everything is light, clean, and pared back to a minimum—enhances the serenity of this room. A tall medicine cabinet offers an elegant solution to hiding clutter, while a huge mirror above the tub adds a whole new dimension of space.**

LEFT **Flooring made from terracotta brick—which can be bought for a song—sets up an interesting visual and textural contrast to glossy white tiles in this utilitarian bathroom, which makes excellent use of natural light. Instead of a dressing mirror, the owner has installed the only item of this type that he really needs: a simple shaving mirror.**

Acquiring a top-quality bathtub doesn't have to cost more than a Christmas shopping expedition. The most important thing is to find a bathtub that's comfortable—so, if you are thinking of buying new, try out various models in the showroom before parting with your money. Traditional white ceramic appliances are relatively inexpensive. What's more, you can find them in all sorts of shapes and sizes. Entire sets are now designed for tiny bathrooms, with corner and sitz tubs becoming very popular. The set doesn't have to match. In fact, investing in one covetable piece, such as a wall-mounted glass or conical wooden sink, can give a bathroom an impressive centerpiece.

Instead of buying a set of shiny new matching pieces, you may want to add interest with reclaimed bathroom fixtures. Scour salvage yards for all sorts of treasures, such as reclaimed bathtubs. If you particularly desire a rolltop, bateau-style tub, make sure the enamel is in good condition, or it many prove expensive to repair. Keep your eyes open for deep ceramic sinks, huge daisy-head

RIGHT, TOP TO BOTTOM **To make toothbrush holders, simply drill holes in blocks of wood. Natural accessories such as a wooden light-pull add individual character to a bathroom. A pebble found on the beach serves as a shower-door handle.**
OPPOSITE **Plywood paneling has been installed to give these bathroom walls the visual warmth of wood. As a modern counterpoint to the reclaimed vanity table, the owners have accessorized with a Philippe Starck faucet and basin for a sleek contemporary look. In the corner, an old enamel bucket makes a good container for other bathroom sundries.**

THIS PICTURE AND INSET **In this funky bathroom, acrylic paint stencils add color and pattern to the wall and the paneled side of the bathtub. A weathered wood block nailed to a wall has become an off-beat toilet-paper holder, while wire-mesh shelves offer an easily accessible, see-through storage solution.**
OPPOSITE **A enlarged photo of blossom has been made into a wall hanging, enhancing the sense of space in this room. Pictures of landscapes and natural objects are a clever low-cost way to create blue-sky horizons in a small room. An old rolltop bathtub has been given a new lease on life with a coat of flat black paint.**

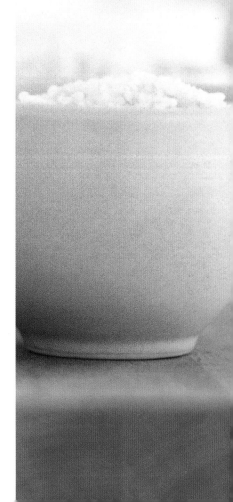

shower attachments, and Victorian toilets. Among other sources of inspiration are used and disinfected hospital pieces—faucets, spouts and cabinets, for example—which perfectly complement a bathroom's sanitary appearance and feel.

A cheap way to keep your bathroom looking stylish is to banish all clutter, keeping only a few beautiful items on view. For a pared-down Zen look, build a closet flush with a wall—this can also be used to disguise an ugly tank. All you need is wood cut to size at your local lumberyard and fitted with push-click closures, so that, when installed, the closet looks like a flat wall.

Another trick is to disguise storage by hiding shelves behind a big brash shiny mirror, or have your basin built into the top of a long, square vanity unit.

For accessories, the most economical approach, as so frequently, is to reclaim, reuse, and recycle. An old butter dish makes a great soap tray; use a pretty vase as a toothbrush holder; employ a rustic railroad tie as a shelf for lotions and potions. Decoration can cost no more than a walk on the beach. Collect objects such as striped pebbles, speckled seashells, and sculptural driftwood and put them on display.

ABOVE AND ABOVE LEFT **Beige mosaic tiles have been used to create stylish waterproof walls. A durable rubber floor like this one is relatively simple to lay and makes an excellent splashproof surface. In the corner, a woven net bag—an inexpensive purchase from a street market—has been put to good use as a child's toy bag.**
OPPOSITE, ABOVE **Compact fixtures specially designed for small bathrooms make efficient use of precious inches in this pint-sized room.**
OPPOSITE, BELOW **Open shelving set into the cabinet doors means that towels and vases are accessible while other less lovely toiletries are stashed out of sight. Shelving installed elsewhere in this bathroom has been cut down from a kitchen work surface.**

top tips for bathing

LET THERE BE LIGHT Make as much use as you can of natural light. Install skylights or extend windows, covering them with opaque blinds.

MAXIMIZE SPACE WITH OPTICAL ARTISTRY Hang a big, light-deflecting mirror near a light; bounce light off shiny surfaces; or dot recessed ceiling lights around the perimeter of the ceiling.

BRIGHTEN UP A quick and simple way to add color and texture to a dull bathroom is to buy colorful towels, bathmats, and shower curtains.

GO DUAL-PURPOSE Stylish radiators make great towel rods, for example—or you could build a storage chest from composite board with a hinged lid that doubles as a seat.

SAVE MONEY, ADD STYLE Scour secondhand stores for classic bathroom accessories. Swap modern faucets for reconditioned originals; find old tile-backed washstands; discover vintage toothbrush holders, soap dishes, and towel rods.

With the personal computer almost as common as the kitchen sink, the "home office" is for many of us the place where we not only work, but also shop, bank, make travel arrangements, and email friends. For others, the home office is simply a quiet place to write letters and pay bills.

There is no getting away from the fact that home computers and associated technology are expensive, but you can save money on the office itself. If you are starved of space, the kitchen table can become a home office by day and a food preparation area at night. A capacious bed makes working from between the sheets another option—with breakfast trays for desks and bedside cabinets for storage. Alternatively, create space. All you need is a hallway end, a nook under the stairs, or a corner of the living room. The ideal is to establish a dedicated work room where you—or your friends or family—can disappear and remain uninterrupted.

The essentials of any home office are a desk and a chair. High-street stores offer low-priced desks in glass, metal, or wood. To save money, buy from office sales, auctions, or secondhand office-furniture outlets. You don't even need an "office" desk: an old kitchen table, an antique roll-top desk, or an outdoor dining table will serve the purpose just as well—or make your own by perching a work surface on trestles, bricks, filing cabinets, or low cupboards.

OPPOSITE **This study occupies part of a living room. In front of the former office desk is an old sewing machine operator's chair, which makes a comfortable seat. Other pieces, including the wire tray, the antique fan, and the old clock, are salvaged from secondhand shops.**
ABOVE RIGHT **The centerpiece of this work area is a drawing board, which has been turned into a desk and paired with a tall stool.**
RIGHT AND FAR RIGHT **Storage is always an issue in office spaces. For smaller storage, use everyday containers such as tin cans, jelly jars, plastic cups, and mugs. For organization on a larger scale, the options include old wooden trunks and box drawers from stationery stores.**

THIS PAGE A fantastic filing system is shut away behind a plastic sliding door, which helps to preserve light and space. See-through filing boxes are both efficient and economical. Buy them for a song at chain stores.

INSET In the London home of two artists, the work area flanks a lime-colored wall. The desk, big enough for both to use at once, is one long bench.

OPPOSITE Occupying no more than an alcove, this home office is a far-from-stuffy affair. With its hot orange chair, yellow cushion and butter-colored shelf, this is a work space that is ready for action. All its features—including specialized desk chair and sensible lamp— put ergonomics first.

A work area is often an integral part of a home.

OPPOSITE This industrial-style home office with its enormous wooden table and metal stools is reminiscent of a genuine workshop. While the ceiling has utility lights for general illumination, a stylish flexible lamp provides adequate task lighting. A galvanized metal floor-to-ceiling cabinet gives plenty of space to stack neatly filed-and-labeled boxes.
BELOW A colorful tin can and a homemade wooden block have become pen holders. Good-looking flower heads in a shot glass add panache.

When it comes to office chairs, it is important to put function before form. To avoid back and neck problems and repetitive strain injury (an inflammation of the wrist joints caused by poor posture), buy an ergonomically designed chair to support your posture. Your feet should be flat on the ground, your wrists at right angles to the desk, and your spine straight. You can pick up low-priced office chairs at sales and auctions, but test them first. Older styles, such as architect's swivel chairs on castors, are office classics and will provide support without making too large a dent in your budget.

Good lighting is another essential. If possible, put your desk under a window so you get plenty of natural light. In the evening, you will need artificial light from a desk lamp, which should be adjustable to provide direct illumination of your work. Most chain stores have reasonable lights at low prices.

The next thing to consider is accessories. You will need storage and shelving for documents, books, stationery, materials, and equipment. For inexpensive shelving, use lengths of bare planks or

ABOVE LEFT The best things in life are free. This trash can, with its lively design, was found by the roadside.
ABOVE CENTER Home offices do not have to look like conventional offices. In this case, a shower curtain on the table makes a protective desk cover—perfect for creative children as well as adults.
ABOVE RIGHT Tiny magnets anchor children's pictures to a cabinet door, softening otherwise steely looks.

LEFT **Any space with a table and chair can be a work zone; this area resembles a sun-filled conservatory.**
BELOW LEFT **Every desk needs plenty of light, so this long bench desk is perfectly placed. The open space underneath is ideal for storage. Among the numerous options for improvised filing solutions are shopping bags, capacious handbags, wicker picnic baskets, and decorated shoeboxes.**
OPPOSITE, ABOVE AND BELOW **First have breakfast, then set the table for a day's work. A trolley on castors complete with office essentials—a phone, files, and printer—is easily moved alongside the desk as needed.**

recycled lumber, or make use of a bookcase bought secondhand. Office sales, auctions, and secondhand stores can be wonderful sources of wooden filing cabinets, plain metal drawer units and metal lockers. While distressed paint finishes are appropriate for a rustic, shabby-chic look, for a smarter appearance you can strip back these once-used pieces and revamp them with a fresh coat of paint or varnish.

For office organization on a smaller scale, you can use glass jars, small vases, or funky glasses for storing pens, while old leather suitcases, doctor's bags, and plastic drawers commonly used to hold screws and nails are ideal for staplers, scissors, rulers, notepads, and other accessories. Other boxes, such as papered shoe boxes, hat boxes, and jewelry chests, make equally chic storage spaces.

As the saying goes, for greater efficiency, you need to "work smarter, not harder." When it comes to cheap chic offices, the key is to spend smarter, not harder. After saving what you can on your office set-up, it's time to splash out on that shiny new all-singing, all-dancing personal computer.

top tips for working

DEMARCATE A SPACE For peace of mind, locate your work area away from other activities. Consider whether you can "reclaim" a room from a hallway or under the stairs, where you can shut the door on work at the end of the day.

GIVE PRIORITY TO BASICS If you don't have a whole room to dedicate to a work space, try a corner of a room, or use your kitchen table, but build in adequate storage nearby.

DOUBLE UP Alternatively, install a fold-out desk in a convenient corner. All you need is a solid piece of painted wood on hinges that can be hidden away in a closet when not required. Freestanding units are available from chain stores, or you can have your own built by a carpenter.

CREATE A LOOK Go retro or Bohemian chic, for example. Team a weathered kitchen table with an old architect's swivel chair, and accessorize with storage boxes covered in floral wallpaper.

THINK ERGONOMIC When it comes to desk and chairs, spend wisely, with your health in mind. It's easy to create a desk—but office chairs have been specially designed to give good back support.

resources

GENERAL

ABC Carpet & Home
881–888 Broadway
New York, NY 10003
For a store near you, call
561-279-7777
www.abchome.com
*Exotic collection of home furnishings,
fabrics, carpets, and accessories.*

Barneys
660 Madison Avenue
New York, NY
212-826-8900
www.barneys.com
Home furnishings and accessories.

Bed, Bath & Beyond
620 Avenue of the Americas
New York, NY 10011
212-255-3550
www.bedbathandbeyond.com
*Everything for the bedroom and
bathroom, plus kitchen utensils, home
décor, and storage solutions.*

Bloomingdales
1000 Third Avenue
New York, NY 10022
212-705-2000
www.bloomingdales.com
*Department store; ,24 locations
nationwide.*

The Conran Shop
407 East 59th Street
New York, NY 10022
212-755-9079
www.conran.com
*Cutting-edge design from
furniture to forks.*

Crate & Barrel
646 N Michigan Avenue
Chicago, IL 60611
800-996-9960
For a retailer near you, call
800-927-9202
www.crateandbarrel.com
*Good-value furniture and accessories,
from simple white china and glass, to
chairs and beds.*

Fishs Eddy
889 Broadway
New York, NY 10011
212-420-2090
www.fishseddy.com
*Overstock supplies of simple 1950s-
style china mugs, plates, bowls, etc.*

Hold Everything
1309–1311 Second Avenue
New York, NY 10021
212-879-1450
www.williams-sonomainc.com
*Everything for storage, from baskets
to bookshelves.*

Home Click
121 Fieldcrest Avenue
Edison, NJ 08837
800-643-9990
www.homeclick.com
*Kitchen and bath furnishings
with a lowest-price guarantee.*

IKEA
Potomac Mills Mall
2700 Potomac Circle
Suite 888
Woodbridge, VA 22192
For a store near you, call
800-254-IKEA
www.ikea.com
*Home basics at great prices,
including assembly-kit furniture, and
stylish, inexpensive kitchenware.*

Macy's
800-BUY-MACY
www.macys.com
*Department store; locations
nationwide.*

Lexington Home Furnishings
P.O. Box 1008
Lexington, NC 27293-1008
For a retailer near you, call
800-539-4636
www.lexington.com
*Designer and manufacturer of wide
range of home furnishings, available
at department stores and designer
showrooms throughout the country.*

Neiman Marcus
For a store near you, call
888-888-4757
For mail order, call 800-825-8000
www.neimanmarcus.com
*Department store; 31 locations
nationwide.*

Pier One Imports
71 Fifth Avenue
New York, NY 10003
212-206-1911
www.pier1.com
*Great furniture and accessories
for every room in the home, including
a wonderful selection of affordable
and stylish drapes and curtains..*

Pottery Barn
P.O. Box 7044
San Francisco, CA 94120-7044
For a store near you, call
800-922-9934
www.potterybarn.com
*Everything from furniture to decoration
details, such as voile curtains,
china, pillows, and candlesticks.*

Restoration Hardware
935 Broadway
New York, NY 10011
212-260-9479
www.restorationhardware.com
*Not just hardware; funky furnishings
and accessories.*

Sears, Roebuck
800-MY-SEARS
www.sears.com
*Leading retailer of home products
and services through catalog, retail
outlets, and online store.*

Target Stores
33 South Sixth Street
Minneapolis, MN 55402
888 304 4000
www.target.com
*A chain store with things both
funky and functional.*

Waverly
800-423-5881
www.waverly.com
*Fabrics, furniture, window treatments,
accessories, and floor coverings.*

FABRICS

Calico Corners
203 Gale Lane
Kennett Square, PA 19348
800-213-6366
www.calicocorners.com
*Retailer of fabric by designers
such as Waverly and Ralph Lauren.
Stores nationwide. Mail order.*

The Fabric Center
485 Electric Avenue
Fitchburg, MA 01420
978-343-4402
*Decorator fabrics at discounted
prices. Mail order.*

Fabrics to Dye For
67B Tom Harvey Road
Westerly, RI 02891
888-322-1319
www.fabricstodyefor.com
*Hand-painted fabrics, dyes, and kits;
available online and from retail outlets.*

Hancock Fabrics
2605A West Main Street
Tupelo, MS 38801
662-844-7368
www.hancockfabrics.com
*America's largest fabric store; good
for all basic decoration needs.*

Laura Ashley Home Store
171 East Ridgewood Avenue
Ridgewood, NJ 07450
201-670-0686
For a retailer near you,
call 800-367-2000
www.laura-ashleyusa.com
Floral, striped, checked, solid cottons.

On Board Fabrics
Route 27, P.O. Box 14
Edgecomb, ME 04556
207-882-7536
www.onboardfabrics.com
*Everything from Balinese cottons to
Italian tapestry and woven plaids.*

Oppenheim's
P.O. Box 29, 120 East Main Street
North Manchester, IN 469-62-0052
800 461 6728
*Country prints, denim, chambray,
flannel fabrics, and mill remnants.*

Pieces of History Antique Linens
76 Cherry Hollow Road
Nashua, NH 03062
www.tias.com/stores/kayhless
*Sheets, tablecloths, napkins, pillows,
bedspreads, and much more.*

Reprodepot Fabrics
917 SW 152nd Street
Burien, WA 98166
www.reprodepotfabrics.com
Reproduction vintage fabrics.

Silk Trading Co.
360 South La Brea Avenue
Los Angeles, CA 90036
800-854-0396
www.silktrading.com
*More than 2,000 silk fabrics;
nine stores nationwide.*

PAINTS & DECORATIVE FINISHES

Chocolate Saltbox Stenciler
1250 Route 171
Woodstock, CT 06281
stencils.hypermart.net
*Largest selection of stencils available
anywhere; over 20,000 designs.*

Color Wheel Co.
541-929-7526
www.colorwheel.com
*Color wheels to help you match
tints, tones, and shades.*

Home Depot
1520 New Brighton Boulevard
Minneapolis, MN 55413
612-782-9594
www.homedepot.com
*Equipment and supplies for every
type of home-decorating project.*

Janovic
1150 Third Avenue
New York, NY 10021
800-772-4381
www.janovic.com
Quality paints in a wide color range.

K-Mart
For a store near you, call
800-635-6278
www.kmart.com
*256 everyday latex paint colors at
moderate prices.*

Lowe's
3909 Ramsey Street
Fayetteville, NC 28311
877-235-6873
www.lowes.com
*Home improvement warehouse,
with paints and wall coverings.*

**McCloskey Special Effects
Decorative Finish Center**
6995 Bird Road
Miami, FL 33155
For a store near you, call
866-666-1935/305-666-3300
www.o-geepaint.com
*The stores carry a huge range of
paints, finishes, glazes, faux painting
supplies, and paint tools and brushes.*

Seamans Discount Wallpaper
166 Spring Street
Dexter, ME 04930
207-924-5600
www.seamanswallpaper.com
*Wallpapers and borders with various
nautical, folk-art, and natural themes.*

Seymour Discount Wallcoverings
10721 Chapman Highway
Seymour, TN 37865
865-577-1181
www.wallcreations.com
*Wall coverings for any room,
discounted up to 80 percent.*

Shaker Workshops
P.O. Box 8001
Ashburnham, MA 01430-8001
For mail a order catalog, call
800-840-9121/978-827-9000
www.shakerworkshops.com
*Manufacturers of Shaker furniture.
They sell Stulb's Old Village Paints
in colors to coordinate with Shaker
tradition.*

Sherwin-Williams Co.
101 Prospect Avenue, NW
Cleveland, OH 44115-1075
For a store near you, call
800-474-3794
www.sherwin-williams.com
*Manufacturers of Dutch Boy paints
and many special lines for specific
stores, such as K-Mart.*

FLEA MARKETS

Alameda Swap Meet
South Alameda Boulevard
Los Angeles, CA 90021
213-233-2764
*Seven days a week from 10 a.m.
to 7 p.m. year round, 400 vendors.*

Brimfield Antique Show
Route 20
Brimfield, MA 01010
413-245-3436
www.brimfieldshow.com
*Brimfield is renowned as the outdoor
antiques capital of the world; show held
for a week in May, July, and September.*

Denver Indoor Antique Market
1212 South Broadway
Denver, CO 80210
303-744-7049
Open seven days a week.

Merriam Lane Flea Market
14th and Merriam Lane
Kansas City, KS 66106
913-677-0833
*Open-air market where estates are
bought and sold; weekly in spring
and summer from 7 a.m. until dark.*

Ruth's Flea Market
Highway 431
Roanoke, AL 36274
334-864-7328
*Over 300 booths selling all types of
collectibles; weekly on Wednesday
and Saturday.*

Sullivan Flea Market
Heights Ravenna Road
5 Miles West of Ravenna Center
Ravenna, MI 49451
616-853-2435
*Antiques and collectibles; held weekly on
Monday from April to the end of October.*

Tesuque Pueblo Flea Market
Route 5
Santa Fe, NM 87501
505-660-8948
*Focuses on Native American crafts,
antiques, rugs, collectibles; monthly
Friday–Sunday. Call to verify dates.*

Traders Village (Houston)
Eldridge Road
Houston, TX 77083
713-890-5500
*Largest marketplace on the Texas Gulf
coast, with over 800 dealers and over
60 acres of bargains. Open year-round
Saturday and Sunday, 8 a.m. to 6 p.m.*

ONLINE RESOURCES

www.amazon.com
*Originally an online bookseller,
Amazon now offers a vast selection
of furniture and housewares online;
many discounted lines.*

www.curioscape.com
*Over 40,000 addresses of stores
selling antiques, including textiles,
throughout the country.*

www.ebay.com
*Internet auctions; every category of
merchandize represented.*

www.fleamarketguide.com
*Listings of flea markets held
throughout the country.*

www.marybethtemple.com
*Linens from the Victorian era through
the 1950s; vintage fabrics and trims.*

www.overstock.com
*Housewares, appliances, bedding,
bath and kitchen accessories available
online at discounted prices.*

www.vintagefiberworks.com
*Vintage clothing, accessories,
fabrics, and home decor.*

www.tias.com
*Vast selection of antiques and
collectibles, including textiles.*

picture credits

All photography by Debi Treloar unless otherwise stated.

Key: a=above, b=below, r=right, l=left, c=center.

Endpapers Anna Massee of Het Grote Avontuur (The Great Adventure)'s home in Amsterdam; **1** Debi Treloar's family home in north-west London; **2** The home of Patty Collister in London, owner of An Angel At My Table; **3l** Susan Cropper's family home in London, www.63hlg.com; **4** Sue Withers & Andrew Moller's apartment in London, designed by Dive Architects; **5** Mark Chalmers' apartment in Amsterdam, kitchen custom-made by Pol's Potten; **6a** Cristine Tholstrup Hermansen and Helge Drenck's house in Copenhagen; **6b & 6–7** Debi Treloar's family home in north-west London; **7r** The home of Patty Collister in London, owner of An Angel At My Table; **8al** Clare and David Mannix-Andrews' house, Hove, East Sussex; **8ar** A London apartment designed by James Soane and Christopher Ash of Project Orange; **8b** Artist David Hopkins' house in East London, designed by Yen-Yen Teh of Emulsion; **9–10** Mark and Sally of Baileys Home and Garden's house in Herefordshire; **11** Annelie Bruijn's home in Amsterdam; **12–13** Debi Treloar's family home in north-west London; **14** Susan Cropper's family home in London, www.63hlg.com; **15l & r** Dominique Coughlin's apartment in London; **15c** Mark and Sally of Baileys Home and Garden's house in Herefordshire; **16a** Anna Massee of Het Grote Avontuur (The Great Adventure)'s home in Amsterdam; **16b** The home of Studio Aandacht. Design by Ben Lambers; **16–17** Sue Withers & Andrew Moller's apartment in London, designed by Dive Architects; **17r** North London flat of presentation skills trainer/actress and her teacher husband, designed by Gordana Mandic of Buildburo; **18** The home of Studio Aandacht. Design by Ben Lambers; **19l** Annelie Bruijn's home in Amsterdam; **19r** Anna Massee of Het Grote Avontuur (The Great Adventure)'s home in Amsterdam; **20al** The home of Patty Collister in London, owner of An Angel At My Table; **20ar** Dominique Coughlin's apartment in London; **20bl & 21** Clare and David Mannix-Andrews' house, Hove, East Sussex; **22al** Mark Chalmers' apartment in Amsterdam; **22ar** The home of Studio Aandacht. Design by Ben Lambers; **22bl** The designer couple Tea Bendix & Tobias Jacobsen's home, Denmark; **22br & 23** Mark and Sally of Baileys Home and Garden's house in Herefordshire; **24l & 25 inset** The home of Patty Collister in London, owner of An Angel At My Table; **26l & ar** Anna Massee of Het Grote Avontuur (The Great Adventure)'s home in Amsterdam; **26br** Annelie Bruijn's home in Amsterdam; **27** Cristine Tholstrup Hermansen and Helge Drenck's house in Copenhagen; **28 & 29ar** Susan Cropper's family home in London, www.63hlg.com; **29al** Annelie Bruijn's home in Amsterdam; **29bl** Debi Treloar's family home in north-west London; **29br** Morag Myerscough's house in Clerkenwell, London—her house gallery/shop; **30–31** Susan Cropper's family home in London, www.63hlg.com; **31l** Wim and Josephine's apartment in Amsterdam; **31r** The home of Studio Aandacht. Design by Ben Lambers; **32l & a** Mark and Sally of Baileys Home and Garden's house in Herefordshire; **32br** Clare and David Mannix-Andrews' house, Hove, East Sussex; **33** Annelie Bruijn's home in Amsterdam; **34al** Nicky Phillips' apartment in London; **34bl** Debi Treloar's family home in north-west London; **34r–35** The home of Patty Collister in London, owner of An Angel At My Table; **36a** Susan Cropper's family home in London, www.63hlg.com; **36b** Cristine Tholstrup Hermansen and Helge Drenck's house in Copenhagen; **37** Mark and Sally of Baileys Home and Garden's house in Herefordshire; **38–39** Artist David Hopkins' house in East London, designed by Yen-Yen Teh of Emulsion; **39r** Morag Myerscough's house in Clerkenwell, London—her house gallery/shop, photograph by Richard Learoyd; **40** Clare and David Mannix-Andrews' house, Hove, East Sussex; **41a** Annelie Bruijn's home in Amsterdam; **41bl** Cristine Tholstrup Hermansen and Helge Drenck's house in Copenhagen; **41bc** Anna Massee of Het Grote Avontuur (The Great Adventure)'s home in Amsterdam; **41br** Wim and Josephine's apartment in Amsterdam; **42** The designer couple Tea Bendix & Tobias Jacobsen's home, Denmark; **43l** Mark and Sally of Baileys Home and Garden's house in Herefordshire; **43r** Nicky Phillips' apartment in London; **44al** Clare and David Mannix-Andrews' house, Hove, East Sussex; **44ar** Mark and Sally of Baileys Home and Garden's house in Herefordshire; **44b** Sue Withers & Andrew Moller's apartment in London, designed by Dive Architects; **45** Nicky Phillips' apartment in London; **46** Mark and Sally of Baileys Home and Garden's house in Herefordshire; **47l** The home of Patty Collister in London, owner of An Angel At My Table; **47r** Clare and David Mannix-Andrews' house, Hove, East Sussex; **48l** Cristine Tholstrup Hermansen and Helge Drenck's house in Copenhagen; **48–49** The home of Patty Collister in London, owner of An Angel At My Table; **49br** Nicky Phillips' apartment in London; **50** Sue Withers & Andrew Moller's apartment in London, designed by Dive Architects; **51** Wim and Josephine's apartment in Amsterdam; **52l** Morag Myerscough's house in Clerkenwell, London—her house gallery/shop; **52c** Mark and Sally of Baileys Home and Garden's house in Herefordshire; **52r** The designer couple Tea Bendix & Tobias Jacobsen's home, Denmark; **53** Sue Withers & Andrew Moller's apartment in London, designed by Dive Architects; **54l** Wim and Josephine's apartment in Amsterdam; **54r–55** Mark and Sally of Baileys Home and Garden's house in Herefordshire; **56–57** Anna Massee of Het Grote Avontuur (The Great Adventure)'s home in Amsterdam; **58 & 59r** Annelie Bruijn's home in Amsterdam; **59l & c** Anna Massee of Het Grote Avontuur (The Great Adventure)'s home in Amsterdam; **60** The home of Patty Collister in London, owner of An Angel At My Table; **60–61** Mark Chalmers' apartment in Amsterdam; **61r** The home of Studio Aandacht. Design by Ben Lambers; **63al** Artist David Hopkins' house in East London, designed by Yen-Yen Teh of Emulsion; **63r** Mark and Sally of Baileys Home and Garden's house in Herefordshire; **64al** Cristine Tholstrup Hermansen and Helge Drenck's house in Copenhagen; **64b** Anna Massee of Het Grote Avontuur (The Great Adventure)'s home in Amsterdam; **65** Wim and Josephine's apartment in Amsterdam; **66l & ar** Mark Chalmers' apartment in Amsterdam; **66cr** Artist David Hopkins' house in East London, designed by Yen-Yen Teh of Emulsion; **66br & 67** Wim and Josephine's apartment in Amsterdam; **67 inset** Mark and Sally of Baileys Home and Garden's house in Herefordshire; **68a** Mark Chalmers' apartment in Amsterdam; **68bl** Debi Treloar's family home in north-west London; **68br** Anna Massee of Het Grote Avontuur (The Great Adventure)'s home in Amsterdam; **68r** Annelie Bruijn's home in Amsterdam; **69** Susan Cropper's family home in London, www.63hlg.com; **70l** Mark Chalmers' apartment in Amsterdam; **70r** Mark and Sally of Baileys Home and Garden's house in Herefordshire; **71** Wim and Josephine's apartment in Amsterdam; **72al** Dominique Coughlin's apartment in London; **72bl** Susan Cropper's family home in London, www.63hlg.com; **72r–73** Sue Withers & Andrew Moller's apartment in London, designed by Dive Architects; **74a** Susan Cropper's family home in London, www.63hlg.com; **74bl** Sue Withers & Andrew Moller's apartment in London, designed by Dive Architects; **74bc & r** Nicky Phillips' apartment in London; **75** Mark Chalmers' apartment in Amsterdam; **75 inset** Susan Cropper's family home in London, www.63hlg.com; **76** Mark and Sally of Baileys Home and Garden's house in Herefordshire; **77al** Clare and David Mannix-Andrews' house, Hove, East Sussex; **77ar & bl** A London apartment designed by James Soane and Christopher Ash of Project Orange; **77br** Susan Cropper's family home in London, www.63hlg.com; **78** Sue Withers & Andrew Moller's apartment in London, designed by Dive Architects; **79al** Mark and Sally of Baileys Home and Garden's house in Herefordshire; **79bl** Mark Chalmers' apartment in Amsterdam; **79r–80l** Artist David Hopkins' house in East London, designed by Yen-Yen Teh of Emulsion; **80c** Anna Massee of Het Grote Avontuur (The Great Adventure)'s home in Amsterdam; **80–81** Susan Cropper's family home in London, www.63hlg.com; **81c** North London flat of presentation skills trainer/actress and her teacher husband, designed by Gordana Mandic of Buildburo; **81r–82l** Artist David Hopkins' house in East London, designed by Yen-Yen Teh of Emulsion; **82ar** Debi Treloar's family home in north-west London; **82br** The home of Studio Aandacht. Design by Ben Lambers; **83** Mark and Sally of Baileys Home and Garden's house in Herefordshire; **84** A London apartment designed by James Soane and Christopher Ash of Project Orange; **84–85** Mark Chalmers' apartment in Amsterdam; **86** Nicky Phillips' apartment in London; **87a** A London apartment designed by James Soane and Christopher Ash of Project Orange; **87b & 88–89** Mark and Sally of Baileys Home and Garden's house in Herefordshire; **89ar** Morag Myerscough's house in Clerkenwell, London—her house gallery/shop. Graffiti painting by Luke Morgan; **89br** Artist David Hopkins' house in East London, designed by Yen-Yen Teh of Emulsion; **90–91a** Cristine Tholstrup Hermansen and Helge Drenck's house in Copenhagen; **91b**

Annelie Bruijn's home in Amsterdam; **92–93** The home of Studio Aandacht. Design by Ben Lambers; **94–95** Anna Massee of Het Grote Avontuur (The Great Adventure)'s home in Amsterdam; **96l & 97b** Annelie Bruijn's home in Amsterdam. Wall spray stencil of deer's head by Barnaby Irish; **96–97 & 97a** Debi Treloar's family home in north-west London; **98–99a** Mark Chalmers' apartment in Amsterdam, kitchen custom-made by Pol's Potten; **99b** Artist David Hopkins' house in East London, designed by Yen-Yen Teh of Emulsion; **100l** The home of Studio Aandacht. Design by Ben Lambers; **100–101** The designer couple Tea Bendix & Tobias Jacobsen's home, Denmark; **102** Sue Withers & Andrew Moller's apartment in London, designed by Dive Architects; **103** Nicky Phillips' apartment in London; **104b–105** Cristine Tholstrup Hermansen and Helge Drenck's house in Copenhagen; **106 & 107r** Anna Massee of Het Grote Avontuur (The Great Adventure)'s home in Amsterdam; **107l & c** Debi Treloar's family home in north-west London; **108l** Clare and David Mannix-Andrews' house, Hove, East Sussex; **108–109** Nicky Phillips' apartment in London; **109r** Susan Cropper's family home in London, www.63hlg.com; **110 & 111r** The designer couple Tea Bendix & Tobias Jacobsen's home, Denmark; **111l** Mark and Sally of Baileys Home and Garden's house in Herefordshire; **112–113** Cristine Tholstrup Hermansen and Helge Drenck's house in Copenhagen; **114 & 115br** Clare and David Mannix-Andrews' house, Hove, East Sussex; **115a, bl & c** Wim and Josephine's apartment in Amsterdam; **116–117** Clare and David Mannix-Andrews' house, Hove, East Sussex; **117 inset** Wim and Josephine's apartment in Amsterdam; **118a–119** Susan Cropper's family home in London, www.63hlg.com; **120l & 121ar** Morag Myerscough's house in Clerkenwell, London—her house gallery/shop; **120–121 & 121b** Annelie Bruijn's home in Amsterdam; **122–123l** Clare and David Mannix-Andrews' house, Hove, East Sussex; **123r** A London apartment designed by James Soane and Christopher Ash of Project Orange; **124–125a** Susan Cropper's family home in London, www.63hlg.com; **125b** The home of Patty Collister in London, owner of An Angel At My Table; **126l** Artist David Hopkins' house in East London, designed by Yen-Yen Teh of Emulsion; **126r–127** Mark and Sally of Baileys Home and Garden's house in Herefordshire; **128** Morag Myerscough's house in Clerkenwell, London—her house gallery/shop, photograph by Richard Learoyd; **129** Debi Treloar's family home in north-west London; **130l & c** Susan Cropper's family home in London, www.63hlg.com; **130–131** Nicky Phillips' apartment in London; **132** Mark and Sally of Baileys Home and Garden's house in Herefordshire; **133** Clare and David Mannix-Andrews' house, Hove, East Sussex; **134** North London flat of presentation skills trainer/actress and her teacher husband, designed by Gordana Mandic of Buildburo; **135** Sue Withers & Andrew Moller's apartment in London, designed by Dive Architects; **136–137** Wim and Josephine's apartment in Amsterdam; **138a** The home of Studio Aandacht. Design by Ben Lambers; **138b** Cristine Tholstrup Hermansen and Helge Drenck's house in Copenhagen; **138–139** Sue Withers & Andrew Moller's apartment in London, designed by Dive Architects; **139r** Dominique Coughlin's apartment in London.

business credits

An Angel At My Table
116A Fortess Road
London NW5 2HL, UK
+ 44-(0)20-7424-9777
and
14 High Street
Saffron Walden
Essex CB10 1AY, UK
+ 44 (0)1799 528777
Painted furniture and accessories.
Pages 2, 7r, 20al, 24l, 25 inset, 34r, 35, 47l, 48-49, 60, 125b.

Annelie Bruijn
+ 31-20-471-0992
annelie_bruijn@email.com
Pages 11, 19l, 26br, 29al, 33, 41a, 58, 59r, 68r, 91b, 96l, 97b, 120–121, 121b.

Archie Cunningham Furniture and Interior Solutions
+ 44-(0)20-8674-1743
www.archiecunningham.com
Pages 15l & r, 20ar, 72al, 139r.

Baileys Home & Garden
The Engine Shed
Station Approach
Ross-on-Wye
Herefordshire HR9 7BW, UK
+ 44-(0)1989-563015
sales@baileys-home-garden.co.uk
www.baileyshomeandgarden.com
Pages 9, 10, 15c, 23, 32l & a, 37, 43l, 44ar, 46, 52c, 54r–55, 63r, 67 inset, 70r, 76, 79al, 83, 87b, 88–89, 111l, 126r, 127, 132.

buildburo ltd
7 Tetcott Road
London SW10 OSA, UK
+ 44-(0)20-7352-1092
www.buildburo.co.uk
Pages 17r, 81c, 134.

DIVE Architects
10 Park Street
London SE1 9AB, UK
+ 44-(0)20-7407-0955
mail@divearchitects.com
www.divearchitects.com
Pages 4, 16–17, 44b, 50, 53, 72r–73, 74bl, 78, 102, 135, 138–139.

Emulsion
172 Foundling Court
Brunswick Centre
London WC1N 1QE, UK
+ 44-(0)20-7833-4533
contact@emulsionarchitecture.com
www.emulsionarchitecture.com
Pages 8b, 38–39, 63al, 66cr, 79r–80l, 81r–82l, 89br, 99b, 126l.

her house
30d Great Sutton Street
London EC1V ODS, UK
+ 44-(0)20-7689-0606/0808
morag@herhouse.uk.com
www.herhouse.uk.com
Pages 29br, 39r, 52l, 89ar, 120l, 121ar, 128.

Het Grote Avontuur
Haarlemmerdijk 68
1013 JE Amsterdam
The Netherlands
+ 31-20-626-8597
and
Het Grote Avontuur Deel 2
Visseringstraat 31
1051 KH Amsterdam
The Netherlands
www.hetgroteavontuur.nl
Pages endpapers, 16a, 19r, 26l & ar, 41bc, 56–57, 59l & c, 64b, 68br, 80c, 94–95, 106–107r.

Josephine Macrander
Interior Designer
+ 31-20-642-8100
Pages 31l, 41br, 51, 54l, 65, 66br, 67, 71, 115a, bl & c, 117 inset, 136–37.

Project Orange
1st Floor Morelands
7 Old Street
London EC1V 9HL, UK
+ 44-(0)20-7689-3456
www.projectorange.com
Pages 8ar, 77ar & bl, 84, 87a, 123r.

SAD Interiors
+ 44-(0)7930-626916
sad@flymedia.co.uk
Pages 8b, 38-39, 63al, 66cr, 79r–80l, 81r–82l, 89br, 99b, 126l.

Susan Cropper
www.63hlg.com
Pages 3l, 14, 28, 29ar, 30–31, 36a, 69, 72bl, 74a, 75 inset, 77br, 80-81, 109r, 118a–119, 124–125a, 130l & c.

Studio Aandacht
Art Direction and Interior Production
ben.lambers@studioaandacht.nl
www.studioaandacht.nl
Pages 16b, 18, 22ar, 31r, 61r, 82br, 92, 93, 100l, 138a.

Tobias Jacobsen & Tea Bendix
www.tobiasjacobsen.dk
Pages 22bl, 42, 52r, 100–101, 110, 111r.

with thanks to:
Echo Design Agency
5 Sebastian Street
London EC1V OHD, UK
+ 44-(0)20-7251-6990
enquiry@echodesign.co.uk
A directory of architects and designers.
Pages 8b, 38-39, 63al, 66cr, 79r–80l, 81r–82l, 89br, 99b, 126l.

index

acknowledgments

Emily Chalmers would like to thank all the owners who let us into their stylish and inspiring homes. Thanks also to Debi, the best photographer and friend, who is a joy to work with. Thank you to Gabriella and Alison at Ryland Peters & Small for giving me another great opportunity and the chance to meet Ali, a gifted wordster and fab new mother; and to Catherine and Henrietta, who put it all together.

Ali Hanan would like to thank the lovely Claire Hector for introducing me to Ryland Peters & Small, Henrietta Heald for her sensitive, eloquent editing, Alison Starling for the opportunity, and Emily Chalmers for her inspiration. I also thank my parents, the Dame and Murray Hanan, and my partner, Dizzy, for looking after our son Luca, who was born halfway through the long birth of this book.